Advance Praise for *The Gift of a Happy Mother*

"Inspiring, heartfelt, practical, and a delightful read! Rebecca's gift to the reader is like a compassionate embrace of a wise friend who's *been* there. She understands the journey, tells you the truth, helps you find clarity, eases your mind, and always sticks up for you."
—Janet Lansbury, author of *No Bad Kids* and
Elevating Child Care

"Today's moms are flooded with social media posts that perpetuate the false idea that they alone struggle with self-doubt, guilt, anxiety, and loneliness. Filled with gentle wisdom, honest revelations, and actionable steps, *The Gift of a Happy Mother* reminds us that the greatest gift we can give our children is our own contentment. Inspiring, comforting, and wise. A wonderful read!"
—Susan Stiffelman, author of *Parenting Without
Power Struggles* and *Parenting with Presence*

"Finally, someone has tackled the stumbling blocks of motherhood—the fear, worry, guilt, sadness, stress and your own inner critic. *The Gift of a Happy Mother* is sterling inspiration. . . . A happy mother is a gift to her child. Make this book a gift to both of you."
—Susan Newman, PhD, social psychologist and author of
*Little Things Long Remembered: Making Your Children
Feel Special Every Day*

"*The Gift of a Happy Mother* is the book we all need. One that lovingly reminds us that we must care for ourselves right alongside our children. This comprehensive look at today's 'joy stealers,' along with easy-to-implement strategies to get it back, will help you feel like yourself again."
—Sarah MacLaughlin, LSW, author of
What Not to Say: Tools for Talking with Young Children

"Rebecca Eanes shares her wisdom and experience, emphasizing why it's important for mothers to cultivate and embrace happiness and fulfillment. She offers self-affirming, practical strategies to help moms build their 'joy armor' and triumphantly navigate the reality, chaos, and challenges of parenthood—and, in turn, empower children to thrive."
—Joanne Foster, EdD, educator and award-winning author

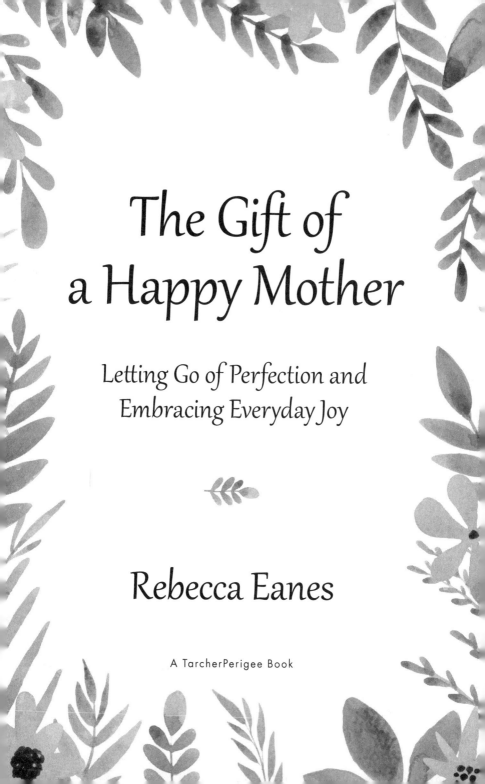

The Gift of a Happy Mother

Letting Go of Perfection and Embracing Everyday Joy

Rebecca Eanes

A TarcherPerigee Book

An imprint of Penguin Random House LLC
penguinrandomhouse.com

Most TarcherPerigee books are available at special quantity discounts for
bulk purchase for sales promotions, premiums, fund-raising, and educational needs.
Special books or book excerpts also can be created to fit specific needs.
For details, write: SpecialMarkets@penguinrandomhouse.com.

Library of Congress Cataloging-in-Publication Data
Names: Eanes, Rebecca, author.
Title: The gift of a happy mother : letting go of perfection and
embracing everyday joy / Rebecca Eanes.
Description: New York : TarcherPerigee, 2019.
Identifiers: LCCN 2018049281| ISBN 9780143131564 (hardback) |
ISBN 9781524705237 (ebook)
Subjects: LCSH: Parenting—Psychological aspects. | Mothers. |
Self-actualization (Psychology) | BISAC: FAMILY & RELATIONSHIPS /
Parenting / Motherhood. | FAMILY & RELATIONSHIPS / Life Stages /
Infants & Toddlers. | SELF-HELP / Personal Growth / Happiness.
Classification: LCC HQ755.8 .E1656 2019 | DDC 306.874/3—dc23
LC record available at https://lccn.loc.gov/2018049281

Printed in the United States of America
1   3   5   7   9   10   8   6   4   2

Book design by Elke Sigal

Contents

In the happiest of our childhood memories,

our parents were happy, too.

—ROBERT BRAULT

For Gavin and Aiden.
You are my gifts.

Introduction

"Would you rather have a perfect mother or a happy one?"

The words that had been swirling around inside my head came tumbling out of my mouth without much warning. It wasn't even that I was striving for perfection—not really. I knew perfection wasn't possible, and yet I did hold myself to unachievable standards, and my inner critic was harsh when I didn't meet them.

It had been a difficult year, which began with a big move to a new state. The village I'd come to count on was gone, our friends and family left behind. My children had difficulty adjusting to the many changes at first, and I worried that we had made a terrible mistake in moving to this new place. Guilt cozied up beside me and whispered of my doubts and shortcomings. Anxiety had become a constant and unruly companion. The happy mom my kids had known was absent, and in her place stood a woman with sad and tired eyes. I hadn't realized that they'd noticed until the question spilled from my lips, and the answer came.

My brown-eyed boy didn't miss a beat.

"A happy one. Definitely."

Something flickered behind his big chocolate eyes as he said it. Longing? Sadness? Perhaps hope? Whatever it was, it caused a stirring within my soul.

Intrigued by his quickness to respond and the assuredness of his answer, I probed further. "Hmm. Would you rather have a happy mom or all the toys on your wish list?" I was half playing with him now, but half sincere. This boy with a wish list a mile long was serious about toys. He had his allowance planned out until his junior year of high school. Surely he'd pick all the toys. That would be his dream!

I was mistaken. To my surprise, he didn't even pause again. "A happy mom," he said more fervently this time. There was a definite hint of hopefulness in his voice now. Oh, my sweet boy. He missed the mommy who smiled. The words he said next still echo in my heart. "I mean, I'd like to have all the stuff on my wish list, but it's more important to me that you're happy."

Wow. This was serious. This was a revelation. I thought for sure he'd choose truckloads of ice cream, candy, and toys, but his heart's desire wasn't for material things. His dream was for his mother to be happy. I suspect this is every kid's dream. To see us laugh. To remember our smile. To feel the joy that permeates the home of a truly happy mother. I long to be what Brown Eyes needs me to be. A happy mom. *I want to wear joy like a suit of armor.* Strong, protective, and secure, I want to live in my shining suit of joy not only so that I may experience sustaining happiness but also that my children will have an example to follow so that they, too, may live joyfully and fulfilled. And so I have set out to build my joy armor piece by piece, day by day, until the day comes when I can look into my sons' eyes and see more than hope, but rather a true reflection of joy.

Each day, I take up my shield and ready myself for the fling of arrows that will come. Guilt. Comparisons. Loneliness. Busyness. Fear. Overwhelm. There are many joy stealers to guard against, but I also have the best reasons in the world to put up my guard. My children. It is my hope that, as they watch me fiercely protect my joy against the slings and arrows of life, they will also take up their shields, build up their armor, and beat back the darkness. It is my hope that Brown Eyes and his brother will always find a reason to smile.

All mothers really want is for our children to be happy. Let's show them how.

This book is being written in the trenches of motherhood, and I write it as much for myself as I do for you. This very morning, my youngest is in bed recovering from a viral illness, and the next few days are jam-packed with extracurricular and end-of-term activities. In the last week alone, I have experienced feelings of fear, worry, sadness, and stress but also relief, joy, gratitude, and contentment. This is real life, Mamas. The ups and downs are inevitable, but we can all strive to enjoy the ride a little bit more. That is why this book exists—to encourage us all to live and love fully through the trials and triumphs of motherhood.

Within these pages, you'll find simple, everyday strategies you can use to build a happier mentality so that you may offer your child one of life's greatest gifts, a truly happy mother. I will provide you with happiness habits, the same ones that I, myself, am practicing. You'll find reflection questions and journal prompts because I've always believed that the best books are books you can dig into and work within, books that challenge you, grow you, and inspire you. I hope this books does all three.

I also want to extend an invitation to you. Please join me in my Facebook community, Positive Parenting with Rebecca Eanes. We are over one million strong, and I'd love to accept you into my tribe. If you're struggling in your relationship with your child, or if you've found conventional discipline practices don't work for you, my books *Positive Parenting* and *The Positive Parenting Workbook* will help you connect heart to heart with your child as you build a loving, respectful, healthy relationship. After all, if you are often butting heads with your child, it's hard to be happy. You can create positive relationships that reduce power struggles, increase cooperation, and add abundant joy to your days.

Let's begin this journey to a happier motherhood. Let's build up our joy armor piece by piece, day by day, until happiness radiates from us and fills our homes with light, touching the loved ones within its walls.

The Gift of
a Happy Mother

Chapter One

Today's Minutes
Are Tomorrow's Memories

Go ahead and look up "how to be happy." Actually, don't bother, because I'm going to tell you what you'll find. Eat nutritious foods. Exercise every day. Get fresh air. Take long walks in nature. Meditate. Find a hobby. Take time for yourself. Read a book. Listen to music. Get up early. Spend time with friends. Play. Do yoga. Practice gratitude. Get enough sleep.

Does that about cover it? I suppose that's solid advice. If you're living at a spa resort with no kids, work, house, or responsibilities to tend to, that all sounds entirely doable. For the rest of us, GET REAL, PEOPLE. I have a little more "free" time now that my kids are older, but when I had littles, I was lucky to get a peanut butter and jelly sandwich scrap and a five-minute shower. Spending time with friends? That'd require a sitter. Listen to music? Sure, if you count the cartoon music. Meditate? Kind of hard to do when someone is tugging on your leg yelling, "HEY, MOMMY!" If chasing a toddler across the play area before he tumbled head over heels counted as exercise, then check. And sleep? You're kidding, right?

Even now that they're somewhat independent and off to school, I'm still finding it difficult to practice all those wonderful happiness habits because, here's the thing, I know what I am supposed to be doing (according to the experts) but *there's something getting in the way.* I'm thinking the key to lasting happiness isn't so much in a yoga pose but in clearing up enough head space to even be able to *think* about yoga in the first place, because that's what it boils down to, isn't it? Creating the space to make those habits part of our everyday routines. The trouble isn't knowing *what* to do, it's *finding the energy and the time* to do it, so that's where we begin—we focus on what's draining our time and energy. After all, one can't learn how to sail the seas if she's drowning in the ocean. A proficient sailor might be shouting all the rules of great sailing to me, but it doesn't matter! Shut up and throw me a life buoy, would you? I'm drowning, for Pete's sake.

That's exactly how I've felt for a while now, like I'll be able to focus on cultivating all those wonderful happiness habits as soon as I get my head above water. Just let me get to safety, then I'll be happy. Still, the waves keep coming and time keeps moving, so it looks like I'd best learn to swim instead of waiting for that buoy. Motherhood itself is a kind of beautiful chaos. The life I knew before has gone, and in its place is wild love like I never imagined and ferocious worry like I've never known. Sure, there is some material clutter that seems to inevitably come with children, but far worse is the emotional and mental clutter that unfortunately seems to also be an inescapable part of modern-day mothering. If I only find happiness in the serene, worry-free, perfect moments of life, I'm afraid I'll find very little happiness. If I am to give my children the gift of a happy mother, I must learn to find happiness amidst the chaos.

Just so you know, this isn't my first rodeo. I've tried to tackle this before, and it went like this: I decide I am, once and for all, going to do everything I must do to be happier. I sit down with my paper and pen and begin a list, because all good things begin with a list, right? I put all the things on this list that I mentioned in the opening paragraph of this chapter because that's what "they" say will make me happy and the Internet can't be wrong. So I then make a notebook of charts for myself because it's good to keep track of important things like this. If I check off a box for the day, I'll know I've done it, and knowing I've done it will make me happier. I have my list and I have my charts. One exercise chart. One meal plan chart. One play chart. One spending time outdoors chart. One meditate chart. One sleep chart. One gratitude journal. How can I possibly fail?

I get up the next morning with all my best motivation but still all of my previous responsibilities, because who is going to take those? That's right. Nobody. So now I have exactly fifty-two charts of boxes staring at me to complete by day's end and I'll be damned if I don't complete every last one so that I can finally be happy. I make that time to exercise really early and, boom, I check off a box. I'm feeling pretty good about myself two hours into my day. That exercise routine took up forty-five minutes, though, so now I'm behind on work. No worries! I'll just buzz right through my writing so I can hurry up and meditate. Only, I can't think of anything except all those boxes to check, and with my mind unfocused on the task at hand, work takes forever. Now I'm really behind. I have to go pick up the kids from school, so I wonder if I can meditate while I'm driving? It turns out that no, I cannot, and definitely not when I have to drive into the crowded, bumper-to-bumper city. Yikes!

I get the kids and rush home (no stops today, boys!) because I have things to do to make me happy, but then, of course, they're hungry. Boys are always hungry, by the way. So now more than half the day is gone and I've managed one happiness habit, which has thrown me way off course. No problem. I'm still motivated. It's just day one. I listen to music while I make dinner because that counts, and I think to myself that cooking can't really be considered a hobby if you despise it, so I probably can't count the fettucine and garlic bread. Fine, so two. I've checked off two now. I exercised and I listened to music. I have exactly five hours left in the day to help my kids with homework, make sure they're bathed relatively well, clean up the kitchen, throw in that load of laundry, go over spelling lists, pack tomorrow's lunches, fold and put away that load of laundry, make myself a nutritious meal because a few bites of fettucine from my older kid's plate surely didn't count, get outdoors for a lovely evening stroll, write in my gratitude journal, play a game with my kids, and get to bed at a decent hour so I can get that proper sleep.

No problem. I'm feeling happier already (sarcasm). I take the dog out to pee and count that as my outdoor time because it's getting late and who has the time for a stroll? Not me. But I checked it off my list and I feel almost good about that. We get homework done, which, by the way, is a fiasco, and I send them off to bathe and pick out tomorrow's clothes while I load the dishwasher and wipe down counters. I think I'm chugging along now at half past seven and then, uh-oh!, I forgot the laundry. I throw in a load and whisper that I am grateful for these dirty clothes because at least that means we have clothes and I figure whispering is basically the same as writing it down in a journal, so I check off that box. It's getting too late to make that poached ginger chicken, Mediterranean tuna antipasto salad, and Asian pear sorbet with thyme (because that's what came up when I Googled healthy meals), so I decide to go for a bowl of Lucky Charms, which at least is gluten-free, so I'm totally counting it. Check. Two happiness boxes left. I've got to play with the kids and get some sleep. But oh, wait, that load of laundry is ready to fold. It'll have to wait, because good mommies play first, right? A meme told me so. Therefore I break out a board game, and if you've ever played a board game with kids you know how long that takes. An hour later, it's time for bed! For them. I still have that laundry to fold, and I should probably shower because I'm smelling ripe from the morning workout, but, hey, all my boxes are checked. Yay! I'm not really feeling happy yet, but I'm sure it just takes a little time or something. You know, like medicine getting in your system. I fold the laundry and put it away and take a nice, warm shower. Now it's 10:00 p.m. and I should be going to sleep right this minute to get a full eight hours, but I haven't checked my e-mail. Plus I need to schedule some posts on my social media business accounts and insert some couple time in there with the hubby. I chat with him about my new charts and he doesn't tell me I'm crazy, which is gracious of him. Finally I crash in bed around midnight. Close enough. Check.

This goes on for three or four days. Each day I'm feeling increasingly more stressed to check off those darn boxes, and I realize this isn't making me happier AT ALL. So I gather them all up in a fit of irritation and chuck them in the garbage can. The critic in my head tells me what an absolute loser I am, and I feel quite sorry for myself for a few days.

At the root of it, my problem was one part overscheduling and two parts bad attitude. I found a lot of places to lay the blame. My children's poor sleep made me tired. My increasing workload made me anxious. My crowded schedule made me resentful. My under-active thyroid made me sluggish. I was good at coming up with plenty of reasons for my recurring bouts of unhappiness until Brown Eyes gave me the kick in the pants that I needed.

This time around, I'm going to start small. Really small. My first step to happiness this go-round is just a tiny baby step. I haven't made a list or checked off a single box. I haven't dedicated myself to two hours a day of happiness habits because that has set me up for failure in the past, and I'm guessing you don't have two spare hours, either. Nope. This time, I've committed to just ten minutes a day.

Strategy: Ten Minutes of Joy

The water sloshed around in the bin as I carried it from the bathroom to the kitchen, droplets splashing onto the floor. I made a mental note to wipe it up before someone slipped. I think moms make about three million mental notes per day. I carefully set the bin down on a spread-out towel on the floor, my three-year-old excitedly stomping behind me. As soon as the bin hit the towel, it was transformed into a giant lake infested with crocodiles and wacky creatures, courtesy of a little boy's imagination. His boat zoomed across the water, Batman in hot pursuit of the villain. Conveniently located to the left of the lake was a building that housed a few jail cells. Several bad guys had already been dealt justice, their blank eyes staring through gray bars. To the right of the lake stood a cardboard town made of varying sizes of boxes covered with construction paper and decorated with the art of four toddler hands. There was a tall purple bank, a short orange church, and several colorful homes. A construction paper roadway provided the citizens of Cardboardville a way into the bustling town where trees grew in random places and people walked their squirrels.

My one-year-old son joined in the fun, running his car along the road. *"Vroom, vroom,"* he squealed as his car crashed through several trees and slammed into the bank. His thin, wispy curls were so adorable, and, oh my goodness, he had a smile that could melt me. He still does. "Whoa! Slow down!" I said, giggling, and I brought my little car alongside his. "Let's race!" I said, and off we went!

"Look, Mommy! Batman got the Joker!" I turned to my firstborn to see his broad smile as he held up the captured foe for me to see before he tossed him into a jail cell. "Way to go, Batman! The city is saved," I affirmed.

It was just an ordinary day, but it produced extraordinary memories that I cherish more with each passing year. The time I spent on my kitchen floor that day playing with my sons didn't seem glamorous or spectacular in any way, and yet it was among the time of those ordinary days where I chose a few minutes of presence that produced the best memories. In those minutes, I was happy. My children were happy. They were the kind of minutes that a joyful life is made of.

Fast-forward to present day and I realize this is exactly what I've been missing—focused blocks of time where I just play, laugh, and enjoy my kids. Since we moved, life has been a whirlwind of deadlines, new schedules, ball practice, homework, housework, and just lots of work. I need to get back to connecting more with my people. Without sufficient connection, we all begin to suffer. It made perfect sense!

> Without sufficient connection,
> we all begin to suffer.

I decided I would start small. I knew from past experience that it would be best not to overwhelm myself with another to-do. I wanted a simple, effective strategy that didn't feel like an added chore, so I landed on ten minutes a day. I determined that for ten minutes, I would put aside everything else and just be present with my family.

I got curious about how just ten minutes per day would impact my own motherhood and my life, so I added up how many joyful minutes I'd gain over the next ten years (until my youngest child reaches eighteen and potentially leaves my nest). I discovered that if I practice joy with my kids for just ten minutes per day, I'll gain 36,500 joyful minutes. That's a lot of happy!

The possibilities are endless. Ten minutes of reading aloud or building Lego creations. Ten minutes of Go Fish or stirring the brownie batter and pouring it in a pan. Ten minutes of snuggling. Ten minutes of listening. Or talking. Ten minutes of undivided attention. It's an *achievable* goal.

Just ten minutes a day equals 36,500 more minutes of happiness during their remaining childhoods.

36,500 more smiles my kids see.

36,500 more minutes of feeling loved, cherished, and seen.

36,500 more minutes of feeling connected.

36,500 more minutes of focusing on those who matter most to me.

36,500 minutes of happy memories.

This has been the single easiest and most effective thing I've done thus far in my journey to greater happiness. It may not seem like much, but small efforts strung together create big change. I've been intentionally focusing on seeing and feeling joy for at least ten minutes each day for several months now, and I know that every block of focused time is building up my joy armor. I feel happier. I am more connected to my husband and kids. I feel like time slows down just the tiniest bit during those ten mindful minutes. Try it out in a very low-pressure way for a week. No beating yourself up if you miss a day. Just aim for a casual, curious mindful presence for a few minutes each day where you notice the laughter, see their freckles, and feel the warmth of a loved one's embrace.

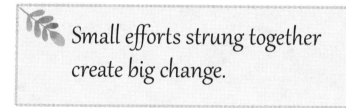

Small efforts strung together create big change.

I feel like I'm not missing out on my life so much now. Just being present and mindful for a few minutes a day is a happiness habit we all can easily adopt. What would ten minutes mean for you? How many more happy memories could you create if you committed to ten joyful minutes a day with your kids?

Happiness Is a Habit

I don't want you to just read a book about happiness. I want you to live and breathe joy in your everyday life. My hope is for you to develop positive habits that lead to a happier, more fulfilling motherhood and life, and so each chapter will feature a happiness habit with everyday strategies you can easily implement, reflection questions with room to write brief answers, and journal prompts so that you can take the ideas presented here and make them your own.

Happiness Habit

Over the following week, as you choose presence and joy for at least ten minutes each day, write down one thing per day that you noticed or observed during that time. What jumped out at you? What emotions rose up? What made you smile?

Day one:

_____

_____

_____

Day two:

_____

_____

_____

Day three:

_____

_____

_____

Day four:

Day five:

Day six:

Day seven:

Journal Prompts

1. How can you create space in your life to make happiness habits a part of your routine? Think in terms of what is holding you back, weighing you down, or keeping you stuck.

2. List just one small, doable action you will take today to create a bit of space. Make it a tiny goal, and then make it happen.

3. What is your *why*? Why do you want to be a happier mom? What would it mean to your children and family? Write your *why* on a sticky note and place it where you will see it often.

4. Write about a happy memory from your past—a day that seemed ordinary when you were in it but produced extraordinary memories.

5. Write instructions on how to find happiness as though you are telling it to a child.

Chapter Two

This Is Motherhood

They tell you that time flies and to enjoy it all you can, and yet in the midst of sleep deprivation, 3:00 a.m. feedings, and endless diapers, it feels like it will last forever. You wonder how time can possibly fly when one night drags on so very long.

Then, one morning you wake up to a running toddler who jumps in your bed and you wonder when she got so big. You chase her around all day until you're utterly exhausted, longing for the rest that night should bring, but it still doesn't come. Unless you've hit a jackpot, toddlers often interrupt your sleep. Still, though, when she throws those little arms around your neck, you wouldn't trade it for all the rest in the world. You have a sense now that what they say is true. The days are long, but the years are short.

You blink, and he's off to kindergarten. It hits you with a nause-ating flutter that the baby days are forever gone and time seems to speed up now. You try to keep up. You do your best to soak it in, but you can't get a good grasp for long enough. He's growing too quickly now, constantly changing, slipping right through your fingers. You can't remember the last time you carried him, when he last rode on your back as you played horsey in the living room, or the last time he climbed in your bed in the middle of the night, but you wish you remembered. You wish you had a picture of each of those moments to carry with you always.

Summers come and go. You know they are numbered, so you pack in as many memories as you can while the days are slower and the daylight lingers. You take lots of pictures on that family vacation, too many according to your kid, but you just have to capture that fleeting moment in time. Now it's back to school, and life once again becomes a flurry of backpacks, science projects, and soccer practices and suddenly they're finishing another grade. Another milestone is reached. Another closetful outgrown.

Before you know it, you're dropping him off at middle school. This boy that you held in the crook of your elbow stands nearly eye to eye with you now. As he walks away from your car, you think he looks too big to be yours. You whisper, *Please let everyone be good to him.* You know how hard middle school can be. And it is. But together, you find your way.

A few more Christmases come and go. Wrapping paper swallows the floor and you relish the laughter that fills your home. You snap more photos and resolve to make albums of every year. You ask someone, "Take one of me with her," because you read an article about needing to be in the photos, too.

The first day of high school brings jitters for everyone, and you realize you're in the homestretch now. You think it's weird how you can still see her toddler face when you're looking right at her at fourteen.

Before you can catch your breath, there are first dates and curfews, cars and proms. Is she ready? Have I done enough? Oh, but you are so, so proud of who she's become, and you are filled with gratitude that she is your baby, no matter how old she gets. She is your baby.

His room is filled with boxes as he packs for college. You know he has to fly, but your nest looks so very bare. Suddenly he's gone, and you stand there in that room as tears escape your eyes. How did it last so long but go by so quickly? You finally print all those photos and catalog your joy by date on sheets of scrapbook paper. Your home is neat and quiet. All that remains of childhood are the photos, memories, and trinkets left behind.

This is motherhood—the unbelievably long and unreasonably short span of loving and letting go. It's the hardest and most wonderful thing you've done and you are forever changed by it all. Your child's fingerprints will one day no longer be on your mirrors, but they'll always be on your heart. Yes, time flies. Enjoy it all you can. Slow down. Catch a breath. Let the little things go. Hold him in your lap. Stay and play a little longer. Connect. Make memories. Great ones. Memories worth holding on to when the little hand you're holding on to now is gone.

As my oldest is finishing up his sixth-grade year, and his first day of high school is a mere three summers away, I'm reflecting on this amazing journey of motherhood, with all of its joys and heartaches. Tear droplets splash my keyboard and seep into the cracks as I type these words because I am overwhelmed with the many emotions that motherhood brings, and I'm also painfully aware of what little time I have left with a precious boy who it seems so recently entered our lives.

This is a reminder to all of you who are now in the trenches of motherhood. You hold your infant and feel like you have a lifetime together. You're bone-tired and so you don't want to hear yet another person tell you how quickly it goes by. That feels like a joke right now. It's hard, I know. It seems like the phase you are in will last forever. I remember the season when I had two tiny ones under my feet all day long, and the days felt very long. The nights were often even longer. It was a season filled with wild emotions, exhaustion, unbelievable joy, discovery, and what felt like a never-ending marathon of diaper changes.

I enjoyed many moments during that season, but I also wished too many away. I used to wish they were out of diapers. I used to wish they'd just sleep through the night. I used to wish for a bit of "me time."

There were nights when I would lie down with them until they fell asleep, and I would be entirely present in that moment, running my fingers through silky hair as I told them story after story. Those were beautiful nights.

Then, of course, there were other nights when I just wanted to be done. I felt frustrated that they couldn't go to sleep on their own, and I questioned every parenting decision I'd made up to that point. I am only human, after all. But just as assuredly as the sun sets each evening, the season that felt like it would never end suddenly did.

That's the rule of motherhood, Mamas. It's all in passing—the hard days, the laughter-filled days, the frustrating days, and the fun days. Everything is temporary. Although there are so many joys to cherish, sometimes parenthood feels so heavy on the heart. It could be from a worrying illness, a child you don't understand, or hurts you cannot take away, but whatever the reason, there will come days when the weight of it is pressing. During the tough days, I remind myself of these five truths, which I share here in hopes that they serve as a reminder to you so that the heaviness may be lifted a little.

1. **My kids are a work in progress.** I know this seems ridiculously obvious, yet I still sometimes feel like the kid in front of me is the finished result. I have to remind myself that they're still growing. Their brains have a lot more maturing to do, and they have a lot more to learn and experience. Who my eight-year-old is today isn't who he will be at eighteen. He's a work in progress, just like me. I believe that the more I find to like about him today, the more there will be to like when he's eighteen. What we focus on grows. So I try to remember to see the good in my kids, even when they're driving me a little bonkers.

2. **Their problems are not mine to solve.** Not always. Of course, I want to help when I can, but they have to struggle through some things. They just do. It's how they learn resilience. Life won't always be fair to them. People won't always be good to them. More often than not, they don't need me to solve their problems anyway; they just need me to be there for them while they work through it, and they need me to believe in their ability to do so. They draw strength from that.

3. **It's never going to be perfect.** It sounds like another obvious statement, but I had some pretty wild expectations when I started this motherhood journey, and I've felt really disappointed to find that it's never *just right*. I've found myself

holding my breath, waiting for the next phase when they'll be more independent or more self-controlled or more mature. I've held my breath waiting for some magical patience potion to appear or a day when a deadline doesn't loom and the house isn't a disaster zone of toys, empty juice bottles, and dog fur. I eventually had to exhale because I realized it just isn't going to happen. There is always something I *could be* bothered about, always something else to wish for. The load feels a little lighter when I decide to find the joy in the chaos.

4. **I've messed up, but they're still okay.** I haven't done it perfectly. Still, there's been plenty of great times, and those outweigh the tough ones. That matters. So, on the days I get it wrong, we talk about it. We listen to each other. We hug and forgive. Then we try again. When you can release the weight of guilt and accept forgiveness, the load is so much more bearable. To the mom who is too hard on herself, you're good enough. Aim for connection instead of perfection. Perfection isn't attainable, but connection heals.

5. **I can't be everything and do everything.** A lot of heaviness comes from trying to do and *be* too much. The kids can put the laundry in. Dad can make dinner. The grandparents can keep them for a night. Someone else can volunteer for lunch duty at school. I don't win a trophy for overextending myself and stressing myself out. So when the heaviness settles in, I take a look at my schedule and my responsibilities. What needs cut gets cut, what needs delegated gets delegated.

Strategy: Buckle Up and Enjoy the Ride

I'm not sure that anyone comes into motherhood fully prepared. It's impossible to know what trials you will face when you choose to bring another life into yours. It's impossible to understand the depth of love until the moment you experience it for yourself. As much as you read, learn, and prepare, you just cannot predict the traits of your children or know ahead of time exactly what they will need. Motherhood requires on-the-job training. It's very much a learn-as-you-go deal no matter how much you think you learned prior to becoming a mom. Arm yourself with grace, humor, and forgiveness. You'll need all three in abundance. Don't forget to notice the beautiful scenery and the exhilarating turns. It's definitely not the easiest, most convenient road to travel, but what a beautiful road it is. Buckle up and enjoy the ride.

Happiness Habit

Abraham Lincoln is credited with saying, "People are just about as happy as they make up their minds to be." Could it really be that simple? Maybe deciding to be happy isn't the only answer, but it sure seems like a good place to start. I think it's something that you have to keep deciding day after day, a sort of unwavering determination to celebrate your life and the people in it. I keep a note in my phone where I continually add advice, quotes, ideas, and inspirations about how I want to live my life. It includes things like "Leave a legacy of love," "Live how you want them to remember you," and "Let them hear you laugh." I look over it regularly.

These days, our devices are never far out of reach. Let's make them tools of encouragement and inspiration. Let them be an aid in motherhood rather than just pulling us away from our kids. Use it to set reminders to take ten minutes to be present. Fill it with notes that point you toward your best self. Collect happy quotes and smiling photos. So often, people let their phones serve as distractions from family. Let's make a happiness habit of using our devices to keep us on track toward the mothers we want to be to our children.

List two ways you can use your device in a way that positively impacts your motherhood:

1.

_____

_____

_____

2.

_____

_____

_____

Journal Prompts

1. Name one way you can enjoy this day just a little more.

2. Do a search for "happiness quotes" and jot down a couple that inspire you.

3. What does your best day look like?

4. Write down a list of characteristics you want your child to see in you.

5. How close is the mom you are to the mom you want to be? How can you get there?

Chapter Three

To the New Moms: Nobody Tells You This Crap

So, you're sitting there with a babe who still fits in your arms and you're being fed loads and loads of bull every single day. I'm going to do you a solid and just be straight with you because I have a hunch that right about now you are feeling a wide range of intense emotions, and all of them are *not* positive ones. You are in utter awe at the depth of your love for that little one, but wow! You had no idea it would be this hard! But who are you going to tell that to? You don't want to seem ungrateful. Maybe you think the rest of us didn't have those feelings or struggle quite that much. Dear new mom, rest assured that we have been there.

You can be grateful for your child but still be overwhelmed. You can be in total love but still feel sad. Every single emotion that is swirling through you right now is 100 percent okay. Your hormones are whacky, you're sleep deprived, and your world has shifted, so honestly, it's fine to feel *all* the feels. You aren't weird, bad, wrong, or unworthy. You're normal! Yes! Normal! If you can't shake the sadness or if you feel overly anxious or depressed, talk to your doctor, but please know that you are not alone and you don't need to feel ashamed.

Becoming a parent is the biggest of all big deals. Your entire universe has been toppled over onto its head and it's no wonder you haven't found your footing yet. Spoiler alert! Motherhood is ever-changing, and just when you think you have the hang of it—PLOT TWIST! It's okay, though. You probably won't find the assured footing you had pre-kid but you're going to learn to dance through life, baby! Dancing is exhausting, yes, but way more fun.

Meanwhile, let's talk about the bull-crap lies you are being handed every single day. We need to expose them for what they are—happiness stealers! These lies make you feel like you're doing motherhood wrong, or like you need to do *more* to get it right because you just aren't living up to standard. Sigh. Those shame monsters of motherhood start chomping at you really early, but we aren't going to stand for it! We are about to get real.

Lie #1: You just need to find balance. Balance is like Big Foot, okay? There are reports of sightings but no one has any substantial proof that it exists. If you get caught up in finding balance, you'll chase that rabbit down a hole of discontentment. I know *some people* make you feel like you should be able to breastfeed on demand for exactly twenty-seven hours a day and still find time to keep your house immaculate, your husband satisfied, and your yoga poses on point. Forget it, sweetheart. If you have a friend who is actually attaining that, I'm pretty sure they'll want her for scientific study because she's not human. Do you know what's good enough? The best you can do for that day. Whatever that looks like! I'm not saying don't reach for good goals. You can inch toward a *more* balanced life without trying to attain the unattainable.

The problem with balance is that it can't be measured universally. My balance doesn't look like your balance because we have different ideas, needs, goals, and lives. Yet, we talk about it like it's this tangible thing that we all should be able to hold in our palms and pet like a baby chick. *Look, I found balance!* It's silly. Some moms feel "balanced" after an hour at the gym, a cup of tea, and a chapter of a romance novel. Others want a night out with friends or a day at the spa. I just want to sleep, honestly. The point is just because some random mom on the Internet says life is all about balance doesn't mean you're doing it wrong because you feel so out of sorts. She's not the Dalai Mama. Instead of searching for the elusive balance, try adopting a more positive mind-set. If I was a betting woman, I'd bet that *balance* is really just another word for looking at the bright side.

Tip: Go buy a goldfish and name it Balance so the next time *that* mom (you know the one) says in the comments section "You just need balance," you can say, "I totally found Balance! It was SO easy!"

Lie #2: If you rub that baby down with lavender-scented lotion, she'll fall asleep in seven seconds, sleep through the night, and wake up dry. Commercials are a joke, and we all know it, but in your sleep-deprived state, you might actually start to believe this should work. You may become discouraged thinking that normal babies actually sleep like that so what the heck is wrong with yours? In reality, if you wipe your baby down in lavender lotion, she'll smell good while she's wailing her head off and keeping you awake. A good-smelling screamer—that's what you get. The best you can hope for is that the lavender scent will give you the slightest bit of calm because you inhale it all night long. I get it, though, I really do. "Your screaming cherub will smell delightful" isn't a great marketing strategy, but it's much closer to the truth. These people are selling you false hopes. Don't buy it.

Bad news: Your baby probably won't actually "sleep like a baby." Studies on infant sleep confirm what you're about to find out and what every mother before you has learned the hard way—babies wake a lot and they usually need your help to get back to sleep. Toddlers may also wake through the night. I had my kids two years apart. Kid number one didn't sleep through the night until he was three. Kid number two didn't sleep through the night until he was also three (at least they were consistent). For one year, I had two children who woke up at different times through the night. I'd get one back to sleep and the other one would wake up. The bags under my eyes had bags. It was hard. Those five years of restless nights sure felt like an eternity at the time, but it seems so long ago now.

Good news: This, too, shall pass. Hang in there.

Lie #3: You'll fall in love instantly and feel an incredible bond with your newborn. Maybe you will, and maybe you won't. Studies have found that nearly 20 percent of new moms and dads feel no real emotional attachment to their newborn. Sometimes it takes days or even weeks, and that can make mothers feel loads of shame and guilt. There are several factors that can interfere with bonding, such as a difficult delivery, postpartum depression, or a previous loss. If you didn't bond instantly, it doesn't mean you're a bad mom! Spend time cuddling, talking to, and getting to know your little one. The emotional attachment will come. Speak to your doctor if you feel like it's taking longer than it should.

Lie #4: Breastfeeding is easy and comes naturally. When I asked a group of mamas what one lie about new motherhood they actually fell for, this was a common answer. Every mother has a unique experience with breastfeeding. Some find it easier than others, and there is no shame in finding it difficult. I wish we could get over the idea that we must check off certain boxes in order to make it onto the "approved mother" board.

Here are some stats. In a study done by the UC Davis Medical Center,[1] 92 percent of the 418 mothers they surveyed reported that they were having problems with breastfeeding three days after giving birth. Half of them had trouble with latching on, 44 percent reported pain, and 40 percent felt like they weren't producing enough milk. Not getting the hang of it right away is completely normal, and one of the reasons mothers give up is this skewed perception that it's supposed to be easy. You may struggle. It's all right not to love it. I had a lot of difficulties and little support, and my babies ended up being lovingly bottle-fed. They're okay. Dust off all that shame and adjust your crown, Mama. You'll be okay either way. Expect it to be hard and maybe you'll be pleasantly surprised.

Lie #5: You need all that baby gear. When I was pregnant with my first child, I created a beautiful, decked-out nursery complete with fancy crib bedding, changing table, magic diaper pail, wipe warmer, and a matching hanging diaper holder. I had baby robes and baby shoes, baby socks and baby towels, baby seats and baby toys. It was pretty insane. My son never slept a single night in that nursery. When he outgrew the bedside bassinet, I moved his crib into our room.

Changing tables are fine, but they're not necessary. A changing pad is really all that's needed (and even that's optional!) because you'll end up changing diapers on the floor, couch, bed, and wherever else there's a bit of flat space. I was not about to drag my sore body up a flight of stairs to change my newborn on the changing table ten to fifteen times a day. Wipe warmers? Seriously? The robe was cute for a photo shoot but otherwise entirely useless. The magic diaper pail wasn't magical at all. Those diapers didn't disappear, and they still smelled terrible. I get the cuteness of baby shoes, but again, until your baby starts walking, no shoes are necessary. Socks were forever sliding off, and I'm still not sure why he needed his own special baby towel.

There is no need to clutter your home space with all that baby stuff and lug it around on every trip to Grandma's and the grocer! Save the clutter for the toddler years. It's coming.

Lie #6: Pull-up training pants will be like your child's first underwear. It is not at all like those commercials where they giggle and shake their booties as they pull them down to go pee pee in the potty and everyone cheers. They lead you to believe your kid will be potty trained in a day with this amazing invention. It'll be *so easy*. Nope.

Here are a couple of scenarios that are closer to the truth. He will pull off this annoying new contraption, which he does not approve of, and throw it on the floor. If you're lucky, he'll do this *before* he poops in it. He'll then run around commando and refuse any and all things that cover the bum. Or he'll use it just like a diaper because it basically feels the exact same to him. Option three is he takes the training pants, tosses it in the toilet, pushes the lever, and says, "Ta-da! All gone! Bye-bye!" Of course, it isn't all gone and you're throwing towels on the floor to catch the overflow. Put that in your commercials, please! Stop feeding us lies of perfect children doing perfect things!

While we are on the subject of potty training, listen. Kids get this in their own time! One day, it might seem like everybody's kid is out of diapers but yours, but trust that your child will eventually get it and don't put too much pressure on yourself or your kid. I stressed over this until I sprouted gray hairs and it didn't make it happen any faster. Save your sanity! Don't worry about it. In the grand scheme of raising humans, this one is not a big deal.

Lie #7: This parenting formula/method/system is sure to make everything perfect! This is the mothership that all the other lies ride in on. The idea that if we do a particular thing, we are assured of a particular outcome is intriguing, but I'm sorry to report that this is fake news. No one can possibly figure out what *one thing* is going to work every time for all our babies, and you should really beware of anyone who claims to have done so. We buy into these lies because we're flipping exhausted and we want some easy answers, for crying out loud. This is too good to be true. There are no guaranteed methods. You'll just have to wing it like the rest of us, sister.

I have only two children, and I have to parent them differently because they are two different people! Kids are unique and so are the parents who raise them. Rely on relationships, not methods. My best advice is to do a little research into child development. Knowing this will save you from holding your child (and yourself) to unrealistic expectations that can totally sabotage your relationship. Research shows parents who better understand child development parent better. It's really one of the best things you can do for yourself, your kid, and your happiness.

Lie #8: You should love every minute. Don't count on it! Motherhood is beautiful. It's amazing, wonderful, spectacular, humbling, breathtaking, profound, and awesome. It's also heartbreaking, challenging, exhausting, and complicated. There's always something to enjoy, but it's not all enjoyable. We all love our kids to pieces, but sometimes we want to run away a little bit. That's perfectly human for you to feel.

Strategy: Lower Those Expectations

The heading sounds kind of bad. Let me explain. I am not suggesting that you go into this motherhood gig with a negative attitude or poor expectations. That won't help you be happier! What I am suggesting is that you be realistic, and I'm not just blowing smoke here. Research says it's true! One study from the University College of London indicates that low expectations is the secret to happiness.[2] Dr. Robb Rutledge, the senior research associate who led the study, said, "Happiness depends not on how well things are going, but whether things are going better or worse than expected."

Your happiness as a new mother (and all throughout life) is really dependent upon your expectations and your perceptions. Shoot for a "realistically positive" attitude, and you'll experience more joy in your life as a mom. "Realistically positive" means that you understand that things will be messy and tiring at times, but you accept where you are on this journey and you look for the joy among the chaos. I found this approach to be really helpful when I had newborn babes in the house. Expecting too much and believing the lies set me up for a lot of letdowns. This strategy will save you a few disappointments during this sweet and perplexing stage.

Happiness Habit

Look for silver linings. When dark clouds roll in or things seem really difficult, look for a silver lining, a glimmer of hope or goodness in the situation. Look for a way to reframe what you initially viewed as negative to something positive or helpful. Do a short, three-minute meditation on that silver lining when you feel it's necessary throughout the day, but try to do it at least once per day.

Let's practice reframing and seeing silver linings! Think of a difficulty from your past. Looking back, can you see a silver lining now? Did the situation help you in some way? Did it teach you something valuable or contain a hidden gift?

Difficulty from past:

_____

_____

_____

Silver lining:

_____

_____

_____

Now think of something in your present that is causing difficulty. What good may come from it? What miracle can you find in the mess?

Negative thought, feeling, or situation:

_____

_____

_____

Silver lining:

Journal Prompts

1. What are some lies you've bought regarding motherhood?

2. Write a list of your emotions out like a grocery list.

3. What are some realistic expectations you can have about this stage of motherhood?

4. How can you develop a more "realistically positive" attitude?

5. What is one thing you are really savoring in this season of life?

Chapter Four

Tuning In to Your Own Voice

Tears spilled down his reddened cheeks again. His bottom lip quivered ever so slightly as he sat in the little green chair at the end of the hallway. I hated the feelings rising inside me, but I pushed them back down and reminded myself that this was what I had to do. Even as the tears gathered in my own eyes, I held my ground because you know all the things they say about children—those wild accusations like "he'll walk all over you if you let him by with things." "He's just trying to see what he can get away with." As though this beautiful, small child had come here with bad intentions. As though he had it out for me. As though he was plotting against his own mother at the tender age of three. Parents often swallow these lies without question, and our children suffer for it.

As I sat there holding my infant son, my heart ached at the turn my relationship with my firstborn had taken. I missed our connectedness. Ever since the new baby arrived, his big brother had been misbehaving. I supposed *the "terrible twos" have just come a bit late,* and perhaps *it is time to begin picking my battles and bracing for power struggles. Discipline isn't supposed to be fun,* I told myself. *I have to be tough. He needs to know who's boss. If I let him by with misbehavior now, imagine how he will act in ten years!* I heard these voices loud and clear in my mind as I stuck to my guns and made my boy sit in that chair for a time-out. I knew the rules. One minute per age; time starts over if he gets up. I was a stickler for rules.

None of those loud voices were my own, of course. They were the voices of family, doctors, and experts that I'd accepted as truth. My own voice was the tiny whisper that I continued to silence and push away. The one that said *Stop this. It's hurting.* Instead of listening to my gut, I allowed everyone else's voices to drown it out. It was only when I finally learned to tune out everyone else and tune back in to my own intuition that mothering became easier, and I discovered I was so much happier when I followed my own heart.

You've probably already realized that everyone has an opinion on how you should raise your baby, and they will share it with you freely and frequently. Ah, the "good ole days" when mothers only received unsolicited advice from parents, in-laws, and a few nosy neighbors. Nowadays, we are bombarded with parenting advice through social media and Web sites. There is a never-ending stream of information available to us all day, every day. The problem is that it has become very difficult to separate fact from opinion and to separate your own opinion from everyone else's.

Having all of this information at your fingertips *can* be a good thing. In fact, in a recent survey I did on my Facebook page, 81 percent of parents surveyed reported that the vast amount of parenting resources available made them happier while only 19 percent felt it was a hindrance. This correlates with research done in the United Kingdom, which found a link to Internet access and well-being and showed that women in particular reap more happiness from Internet use, though the report didn't explore why.

My guess for the reason in the uptick of women's happiness in that study is that Internet access enables us to connect with others, find like-minded friends, organize our households, and laugh at hilarious cat memes. The Internet can inspire, motivate, and enlighten. Certainly the World Wide Web has been instrumental in my journey as a mom and led me to information that helped me make significant, positive changes in my parenting style and relationships. It has provided me with new friends and an amazing support system. Some of my very closest friends live in countries very far away, and I never would have known these beautiful souls if it wasn't for Internet access.

Yet there is a dark side to having unlimited information at your fingertips *and* to people having basically unlimited access *to you*. The nonstop voices can clutter your head and drown out your own. They can make you second-guess your decisions and feel like you're doing everything wrong. The Internet gives us more moms to compare ourselves to and subjects us to "sanctimommies" whose voices scream, "You are not as good as me!" You can be trolled, harassed, shamed, and condemned for your mothering choices, and these can be deeply painful experiences. "Our era," says author Greg McKeown, "is distinguished not so much by information overload, but by opinion overload. To ensure that our own voice is not lost in the noise around us, we need to know what we want."

Strategy: Define What You Want

And so, Mama, that is the first task at hand for this chapter—to define what it is that you want. When you get crystal clear about exactly what you want, what you believe, and *why,* your own voice will be able to rise above all the others and lead you. You cannot align to your truth until you know what your truth is, and so begin with the happiness habit and journal prompts that follow to discover your truth. I highly recommend that you do these activities in an uninterrupted time of stillness. I know those are hard to come by.

Happiness Habit

Build a "quiet the mind" habit into your daily routine. This does not have to be an hour-long meditation ritual or another box to tick off in your day! Begin with three to five minutes a day of sitting or lying comfortably and focusing on the sensation of your breaths. Do not try to think of answers or call up your purpose, but simply allow your mind to rest. This is not a time to seek out anything but simply a time to just sit with yourself and *be.*

Learning to quiet the constant chatter in your mind is a major step toward tapping into your intuition, and this simply requires practice to master. Feel free to record your progress regarding this exercise over the next week. As you sit in stillness, jot down what thoughts keep coming up that you must quiet. Write how you feel afterward. Make note of the time spent and the ease at which you completed the exercise. All of this information will help you to master this important skill.

Day one:

_____

_____

_____

Day two:

_____

_____

_____

Day three:

_____

_____

_____

Day four:

_____

_____

_____

Day five:

_____

_____

_____

Day six:

Day seven:

Journal Prompts

The following questions will help you gain clarity as to what you want in your mothering journey.

1. What is one gift you want to give your children?

2. What did you need when you were a child that you received and what did you need that you didn't receive?

3. Write a list of adjectives: Mothers are . . .

4. When your children describe you to their children, what do you hope they say?

5. Name one thing you know you need to work on.

Why Your Gut Is Supersmart

Did you know that you have more than one hundred million brain cells in your gut? Your enteric nervous system is a system of neurons that governs the gastrointestinal tract and is sometimes called "the second brain." It is in regular communication with your central nervous system. If you've ever had "butterflies in your stomach," that was your brain and gut talking back and forth. This may provide an understanding as to why we have a "gut feeling"; perhaps our gut understands what's going on at a subconscious level just as our brain understands what is going on in our microbiome.

In addition, scientists have discovered that we appear to have two operating systems. According to Kelly Turner, PhD,[3] the first is controlled by our right brain and parts known as the "reptilian brain." It's instinctual, quick, and often subconscious, while the second is the slower, conscious, analytical system controlled by our left brain and the neocortex. Intuition is part of that first instinctual system. Turner says, "In other words, intuitive decisions are not something that we have thought out carefully with reason, but rather choices that have arisen quickly out of instinct." Furthermore, researchers have found that our first system often knows the answer well before our second system, and most often, our "gut instinct" is correct.

Studies have shown that, when it comes to making major decisions (and most parenting decisions feel major!), trusting your gut leads to better outcomes. Long story short—that gut feeling you get is going to serve you better than the Nosy Nancy in your moms' group. You can't argue with science!

Remember my story at the beginning of this chapter? The one

where I was stuck in a cycle of time-outs and tears with my son? Well, every time I placed him in that chair and left him alone, my gut told me it was wrong. I ignored it for months. It turns out, my gut was totally right about it.

My boy wasn't being defiant or naughty; he was processing big feelings about having a baby in the house who took up so much of his mommy's time, and he was sad because he and his mommy had been so very close. Listening to the outside voices caused me to miss something very important—my child's distress. I was so focused on behavior that I didn't see the pain at first. I saw what I expected to see. Terrible twos. A defiant toddler. A kid vying for control. That was completely wrong. Once I listened to my intuition and looked at what my son was experiencing, I learned that he has the trait of high sensitivity, and all he needed was connection and gentle direction. I'm thankful that I decided to finally listen to my gut and found our way out of that messy cycle.

Sprinkled throughout the story of my motherhood are many, many instances when I was unsure of the choice I was making. Many times I've shushed my gut because my thinking brain took over and thought it had all the answers, but I can't think of a single time when I was glad I didn't follow my gut. Distinguishing my inner voice from the world's loud voices has not always been clear or simple, but at least now I've learned to stop and listen to my gut, because more often than not, it guides me in the right direction.

Strategy: The Gut-Feeling Check

Learning to listen to a quiet voice in a very noisy world can be challenging. Any time one of my boys is having a hard time making a decision, I tell him to flip a coin. No, it's not about heads or tails. I tell him that he'll hear the answer when the coin is in the air. It's whatever he's hoping it lands on. It's a pretty neat trick. Try it the next time you are agonizing over a decision.

Be open to what your intuition is telling you. Sometimes I'm afraid it's going to tell me something I don't want to hear. Sometimes following an expert's advice feels safer. It can feel scary to follow something as abstract as a gut feeling, but maybe knowing that it is your second brain will help you feel a little safer.

Happiness Habit

My thinking brain likes to think—a lot. You might say it's a little overzealous. If I allow myself to start analyzing my gut feeling, I start feeling totally confused. Don't try to throw logic in there. This chapter's happiness habit isn't one to start but one to break.

Break the habit of overthinking everything. Overthinking is a happiness stealer and zaps so much energy. It can make you feel exhausted and overwhelmed. Just go with what you initially felt was right and see how it pans out.

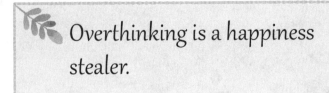

Overthinking is a happiness stealer.

Journal Prompts

1. Remember a time you didn't follow your intuition. What was the outcome?

2. Remember a time you did follow your gut feeling. What was the outcome then?

3. Is there anything you have a hunch about now that you should listen to?

4. What fears do you have about following your gut?

5. How would you describe how a gut instinct feels to a child?

Chapter Five

But I'm So Busy!

A few years ago, I was really busy. Not your average, everyday busy, but ridiculously busy. On the outside, I looked like a really productive supermom. I wasn't just keeping up with the Joneses, they were eating my dust! I could homeschool my kids, run a Cub Scout den, teach co-op classes, organize field trips for our group, write books, publish blog posts, grow a social media following for my business, put together fun sensory and/or educational play invitations for my kids, cart my kids to karate lessons, and keep my house looking pretty decent. Psssh. All in a day's work. Can you guess how this story ended?

In an emotional breakdown. That's how. Who would have guessed? I may have looked like supermom, but behind the facade was a tired, irritable woman who wasn't giving her best to her family. My anxiety was absolutely through the roof and depression was knocking at my door because that is the disease of busy. It slowly eats at you until you don't really recognize yourself anymore. You get so busy *doing* that you forget about *being*.

Why do we take so much pride in being busy? Why do so many people wear it like a badge of honor? Why did *I* wear it like a badge of honor? For some of us, being busy makes us feel important, valuable, needed, and worthy. Others hide behind their busyness, desperately trying to mask the turmoil of their private lives with a to-do list. All of those boxes to check occupies the mind, and sometimes it's easier to be lost in the hustle than to sit with ourselves in the quiet. For me, it wasn't that I wanted to feel important; I just wanted to feel like I measured up. Everyone in my circle had a full plate and handled it gracefully. They were always volunteering and always smiling, carrying a baby in one arm and a plate of beautifully decorated made-from-scratch cupcakes in the other. They seemed to have it all together, and I didn't want to feel like the loser who couldn't keep up. I think proving our worth, whether to ourselves or to others, is so often at the root of our busyness.

For me, though, keeping up came at a high cost. When I finally took off my mask, I began to wonder how many of those other supermoms were wearing one, and what they really looked like underneath, because underneath my mask was a tear-stained face with mascara streaks, dark circles, and a scowl. I had all I'd ever wanted and found very little joy in any of it, and that is no way to live life, my friend. After spending all that time and energy, it turns out that I didn't prove my worth to one single person. Not one. I was just another dog in the race, and no one was paying attention to my accomplishments. They were too focused on their own. The people who really mattered knew that my worth wasn't attached to my accomplishments, and to my two little boys, it didn't matter how much I hustled. They didn't want a highly esteemed mom or a polished mom or a supermom. They just wanted a happy mom.

There's another issue at play here, one that cannot be ignored. We have become so accustomed to constant stimuli that in the absence of it, we feel uncomfortable. We self-create much of our own stress and busyness because it's more comforting to us than sitting still. In a series of studies, participants were left alone in a room for up to fifteen minutes and reported not liking the alone time. They were then given a mild shock and asked if they'd pay money to avoid being shocked again. The participants said they would pay to avoid pain, and yet those same participants, when left alone in a room for fifteen minutes a second time, chose to voluntarily shock themselves rather than just sit there with their thoughts. Isn't that . . . shocking? Some of us can't stand not being busy even though it creates stress. Stress is sometimes more familiar and comforting than stillness.

Then, of course, there's the people pleasing. Do you hate to disappoint others? Me, too. I want everyone to like me, and I want to make everyone happy, often at the expense of my own time, energy, and happiness. Wrapped in my people-pleasing tendencies is an entanglement of perfectionism, a fear of rejection, and a very real need to feel worthy. Our drive for belonging can lead us down a very treacherous path if we aren't careful, because when our own needs go unmet, resentment builds and even the tasks we initially found joy in taking on become a joyless drag.

A few years ago, I would have gone to great lengths to feel like I could measure up to the other moms, but eventually I got tired of sacrificing my happiness at the altar of busy. I decided it wasn't worth the hassle to me or my children to keep doing it all and being it all, so I drastically pared down my commitments and our schedule. In fact, I probably went a little too far in the other direction because I darn near went into hibernation, but it was needed at that time. Did I let down a few people along the way? Yes. It felt uncomfortable to let people down, but I was finally putting my family first, and that actually felt really good. Saying no to other people didn't cause the world to collapse after all.

Happily Busy or Hustling for Worth?

Let's be clear. Not all busyness is destructive. There's the "hustling for worth" busyness like I just described, but there's also the kind of busy that is joyful and fulfilling rather than overwhelming and draining. My little family is currently in a "happily busy" season filled with things we all enjoy doing. There are still down days built in, and we have created some cozy family rituals along the way that require us to slow down and be together. That's been the key to finding joy in busyness.

It's one thing to be busy doing the things you love—the things that feed your soul and give you joy. It's quite another to be miserably busy, stressed, overwhelmed, and drained. What's your busy status? Are you happily busy or are you hustling for worth? Before, I was constantly trying to pour from an empty cup. Now, when I feel my cup running low, I take a little extra time to fill it back up. Doing that wasn't easy when my children were very young, so if you're in a situation that doesn't allow you much "me time," please accept this through-the-book hug. There's almost always a way to refill, though, Mama. I know that I spend time each day scrolling through social media feeds that I could spend sleeping or reading a good book. You, too?

Happy mom tip: Don't allow your busyness to cause you to miss out on the things that truly matter in life. It's difficult to be in the present moment with your children when your mind is racing or you are physically on the go. You might be missing out on an important conversation your teen needs to have or on playing with your toddler. You might be missing out on a special moment with your partner or a chance to love someone in their time of need because you were too busy to see the invitation. I've certainly been guilty of doing those things, and I'm willing to bet most of us have, but this isn't about perfection! It's about mindfulness and increasing happiness. It's about loving the ones we are with and putting down our phones, our schedules, and our distractions.

Mama, you've got to know that your value is not tied up in the brownies you make for the bake sale or in your ability to volunteer to work the book fair. It's not tied up in how many e-mails you get answered or how quickly you meet that deadline. It does not hinge on how many words you write, how many products you sell, how many steps you take, or how spotless your house is. It's not measured by extravagant dinners, amazingly cute birthday parties, or anything that you can or cannot create. You are a valuable mother. You were born worthy of love, belonging, and happiness, and if you didn't get those in your young life, I am truly sorry. You didn't have control over the first chapters of your life, but you have control now. Your children think you hang the moon, and what matters most to them isn't your accomplishments but your presence. They just want to be with you, to be held by you, to hear you laugh. Your kids see your value, and it's about time you see it, too.

> Your kids see your value, and it's about time you see it, too.

Strategy: Collecting Miracle Moments

Each day contains miracle moments—small (or big) moments in time that bring us joy, awe, happiness, contentment, and wonder. These are the moments that take our breath away, that enliven our spirits and warm our hearts. If we stop long enough to collect these passing moments—to notice and appreciate them—these miracle moments will increase our happiness just by way of gratitude.

Why does this strategy make a difference? It interrupts the busyness cycle long enough for you to pay attention to the beauty and goodness around you. This mindfulness exercise will help you start to engage more with your life and your loved ones rather than simply going through the motions of busy. Research on mindfulness shows that daily practice improves health, decreases our vulnerability to stress, improves emotional intelligence, and, yes, increases happiness!

I recommend keeping a jar filled with your miracle moments. Each time you collect a miracle moment—a child's laugh, a loved one's embrace, a warm bed, a cup of tea, a bird singing—jot it on a slip of paper, fold it, and put it in your jar. It's a tangible way to see your happiness rising as the jar fills to the top with life's joys.

Happiness Habit

Think of three miracle moments that happened today. Write them here.

Journal Prompts

1. Are you happily busy or hustling for worth? How is your busyness serving you?

2. What are things you'd like to say no to?

3. Write out your current commitments and then cross out the ones that aren't bringing you joy or goodness. What's left?

4. Write a list of your priorities. Are the things you are spending your time on reflecting your priorities?

5. What is the worst that could happen if you decide to just say no or end the commitment?

Chapter Six

Brain Bully:
Wrangling Negative Thoughts
and Attitudes to the Ground

Do You Know Debbie?

From the outside, it seemed that Debbie should be very happy. She had a doting husband, three great children, a nice home in the suburbs, and a career she worked hard to achieve. Yet Debbie was never satisfied. She knew she *should* be happy, but she always saw the glass half empty. Even though her husband was kind, hardworking, and a good father, she was constantly annoyed by his late hours at the office and his woodworking hobby, which she thought was a waste of time. Her children were eight, six, and two, and although she loved them fiercely, they wore her out. There was no such thing as relaxing after work for Debbie. There was only homework, lunch packing, sibling squabbles, dinner, and story time. By the time her husband got home at around 8:00 p.m., she was usually cranky and in a sour mood.

She thought if only her husband was around to help more, she'd be happier. If only the children were more independent, she'd be happier. If only they could afford a nice vacation, she'd be happier. If only she could get to the gym and lose those stubborn pounds, she'd be happier. If only her vehicle was paid off, she'd be happier. If only she'd get that promotion . . .

Time passed, and her children grew. Now sixteen, fourteen, and ten, they were more independent for sure. A little *too* independent if you asked her. Raising two teenagers and a preteen meant constant worrying for Debbie. She wished often that they were little again and regretted that she didn't enjoy them more when they were younger. Her husband had since taken a new nine-to-five job and was home just minutes after she arrived, but even though he was around to help out more, her attitude hadn't really changed. She still had too many responsibilities, and there just weren't enough hours in the day to get everything done.

She thought if only she could sleep better, she'd be happier. If only she could go back and start over, she'd be happier. If only she knew her children would make good choices and be successful, she'd be happier. If only she didn't have to worry about how to help her child pay for college in two years . . .

Her home became eerily quiet. Her youngest child had moved out more than a month ago. She sobbed underneath a blanket in the last room to go empty, filled with so many regrets. What she would give to have them all back home, just babies once more. She'd make time to play. She'd worry less. She'd enjoy their laughter instead of fretting about bedtimes and messes made. She'd pay more attention to the little details that she was finding harder and harder to remember—the way they had smelled nuzzled against her chest, the dimples at the knuckles of their toddler hands, the sound of their voices before they'd all changed. Looking at her husband, she realized she'd not truly seen him in years. She wished he didn't feel like such a stranger to her now. She felt so lonely.

If only she had held them more, she'd be happier. If only she'd said yes to playing dolls and trains and dress-up instead of "Not now, I'm busy," she'd be happier. If only she felt connected to her husband, she'd be happier. If only she could finally retire, but that's still a decade away . . .

Her smooth skin became aged, her furrowed brow showing decades of worry. Her graying hair cascaded down her shoulders as she lay in the hospital bed alone. She knew her children would be there in the morning, and she smiled a weak smile at the thought of seeing them. Her health was failing and the outcome was unsure, but there was one thing she desperately wanted to tell her children. When they all gathered around her, she said:

Live each day with a grateful heart. Do not wait to be happy someday. Enjoy your children while they are young. Put down your devices and your priorities for a while and look at them. Really look at them. Say yes when they ask you to play. Notice their dimples and curly locks. Don't fret too much about the little things, for they are little, after all. Life is long, but also fast, and when it's over, it's done. You can't go back. Live and love well today so that you don't live with regrets tomorrow. Make beautiful memories and hold on to them, and most of all, be happy. Just be happy.

I don't only *know* Debbie, I've *been* Debbie. I don't want this to be my story, and yet I have found myself looking through Debbie's eyes. I've missed the beauty in my life because I was staring at my problems. I've let many joyful moments slip through my fingers because of a negative attitude.

In this example, even though Debbie began having regrets when her children were teens, she still didn't take the time to enjoy the season she was in. She only had regrets for the past and fear for the future; no love for the present. It's an unhappy state to live in. I don't want to live my life with a negative attitude and miss the joys that are right in front of me.

I know that if I want to give my children the gift of a happy mother, I need to be mindful of my attitude. As long as I can remember, I've struggled with negative thoughts. However, I've done enough research to understand the importance of developing a positive attitude to help me be a better, healthier mom. A positive attitude, though, is more than plastering on a fake smile and forcing myself to dance when I really don't want to. It involves real work on my thought processes, how I see the world around me and the people in it, and my ability to surf the rough waves and to get back up when I get knocked down.

Neuroscientists give us good news and bad news, of course. I'll tell you the bad news first. Toxic negative thoughts are addictive. Those bad thoughts give us a little hit of the same stuff we get when we indulge in any addictive behavior. In addition, our brains are evolutionarily wired to focus on the bad. It's trying to protect us, so we can't hate on it too much. Our ancestors needed to be focused on the dangers around them to stay alive. There's more bad news. Once we get into the loop of negative thinking, the neural pathways that have formed make it easy to return automatically to these thought patterns. Oh, and one more thing. Ruminating on the negative stuff can damage the neural structures that regulate emotions and memory.

Here's the good news. Our brains are changeable, and, with a good deal of honest effort, we can rewire our brains to be more positive and optimistic. Thanks to experience-dependent plasticity, when we change our experiences (our thoughts and how we perceive what happens to us), we can change our neuronal structures. Over time, it gets easier and easier to think positively. Positive thinking is linked to better health, longer life, reduced stress, lower risk of depression and cardiovascular disease, and loads of other good stuff. It really is worth the effort.

Our attitude is a choice, even though it doesn't feel like it. Nobody gets to write your story but you. You determine how your life will go, and here's the kicker for us moms. The same is true for our children! We want our kids to think positively and have a good attitude, but who are they always watching? Who are they learning all about life from?

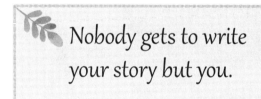

Nobody gets to write your story but you.

It's a twofold issue. One—children learn how to deal with the ups and downs of life by watching their parents. They often adopt our attitudes. In turn, of course, their own attitude determines how their lives will go and their own happiness level. So we want to set a good example for them to follow. Two—Mom's mood sets the emotional tone in a home. How I feel affects everyone in my family. I haven't read a study on this, but I can see it's true in my house, and I bet you see it, too. "If Mama ain't happy, ain't nobody happy" is generally truth around here.

Strategy: Challenge Your Negative Thoughts

So how does someone create new neuronal pathways? You have to get fierce! Hold each negative thought up to the light and watch it squeal. They hate light because most of them are dark lies. Stop the negative thought, yes, every single one, and challenge it. Is it true? Then, replace it with a good thought, or at least a neutral, accurate thought. This is a difficult, time-consuming process, and it doesn't happen overnight. You might challenge negative thoughts hundreds of times per day at first! It can be tedious, but look at it this way: You're already having thoughts all day anyway, so you may as well be doing something useful with them!

Happiness Habit

Challenge a few of your common negative thoughts in the space below.

_____

_____

_____

_____

_____

Positive thinking will let you do everything
better than negative thinking will.
—Zig Ziglar

Journal Prompts

1. If your child was having negative thoughts, what would you advise?

2. When you think positive thoughts, what do you feel in your body?

3. How does your sour mood affect your children? What do they do?

4. List five things that bring you peace.

5. List five things that bring you joy.

Standing Up to the Bully in Your Brain

"You look gross," she said. Her eyes narrowed, her nose crinkled in a look of disgust. She didn't break her stare. Then, she threw another punch. "You've aged ten years in the last month. Look at those lines." My heart sank, and I walked out of the bathroom to get away from the jerk in the mirror.

Of course, she followed me. She followed me everywhere I went, teasing and mocking often.

"Nobody cares what you have to say."

"You're a joke. Give it up."

"You have zero talent."

I came in contact with my fair share of bullies throughout childhood, but none as formidable as the one who resided inside my own head. My inner critic was large and in charge before I tackled this happiness stealer on my journey to being a happier mom. The truth is, I didn't like myself very much. I wouldn't have liked anyone who talked to me that way, so that was certainly understandable. Sometimes the biggest critics we face in our lives are ourselves.

I could go on about the kids in school who called me "hippopotamus" or how my work has been criticized as recently as two days ago. We all have stories like that, don't we? I could blame them all for the harsh voice inside my head, but placing blame doesn't fix the problem. In the end, this is my show, and I decide who'll be the star. There will always be people in the world who don't see our value. It's when we stop seeing it ourselves that's the real problem.

The first time my son received a hateful comment on YouTube, I told him this. "Don't let someone's hateful spirit invade your beautiful heart and soul. They can't see your light because they live in darkness. That doesn't mean you aren't shining, though. Shine on." I give him different versions of this same message every time someone fails to see his light. I don't ever want him to lose sight of his value. Saying this to him stirred up a lot of emotion in myself, and I realized my heart desperately needed this message, too.

To the girls in elementary school who teased me, to the boys who dumped me, to the friends who backstabbed me, to the Internet critics, to everyone who has said a hateful word about me, and especially to the bully in my brain, hear this: Your hateful spirit will not invade my heart and soul. I will shine on.

Strategy: Hush, Little Critic, Don't Say a Word

Dealing with inner bullies is a lot like wrangling down those negative thoughts, but it's more personal. A negative thought might be *This day is a total failure,* but the inner bully might say, *You are a total failure.* Stop those hateful thoughts about yourself in their tracks and start saying positive things about yourself every day, even if it feels ridiculous at first. Positive self-talk will build your self-esteem and confidence. When that inner critic rears her ugly head, say, *Hush, little critic.* Then remind yourself how awesome you are, because, Mama, you're incredible!

Happiness Habit

Write a friendly letter to yourself. List your good qualities and tell yourself why you are worthy of love and joy.

Journal Prompts

1. Write down some specific messages that your inner critic tells you.

2. Write your intention for overcoming negative thoughts and attitudes. What is one specific action you are going to take?

3. What makes you feel proud of yourself?

4. What is something that you're good at?

5. What do you need to forgive yourself for?

Chapter Seven

Toxic People and Habits

Did someone's name immediately come to mind when you read the chapter title? It's usually clear who the toxic people are in our lives. What isn't always clear is how we should handle them. When the toxic person is a family member or a colleague you cannot easily get away from, it's even more difficult to stop the draining of your happiness. However, because our children will one day be faced with a toxic person in their own lives and must then choose whether to be drained or draw the line, I believe we have not only the right but also the responsibility to create healthy boundaries.

While most toxic people are obvious, some are tricky. Here's the test: Do they leave you feeling emotionally drained, angry, argumentative, shamed, self-critical, or depressed, and does this happen frequently? Having a bad day or going through a rough season doesn't necessarily make a person toxic. We are all human, with flaws and weaknesses that we need to be loved in spite of. However, a relationship becomes toxic when you are repeatedly negatively affected and your boundaries are not being respected.

The big question is: *Where do you draw the line?* This is a difficult question, and so many will tell you to cut out the difficult people in your life immediately and don't look back. Toss them aside. Forget them. Sometimes, I do believe that is necessary, but let's not be too quick to toss people away like dirty sponges. It's really easy to love the lovable people, the people you jive with, the people who sing your song. But the people who rub you the wrong way, the negative people, the difficult people—are they unworthy of love and relationships? I think the ones who aren't very good at loving are the ones who haven't been loved very well. These people call for boundaries, absolutely. They cannot be allowed to mistreat you, but they can be flawed and wounded and imperfect and still deserve to be loved and to be a part of someone's life. And maybe when you give these hurting people a second chance, forgiveness, love, and kindness, it will make them hurt a little less. Maybe you have a part to play in their healing. So, let's make careful decisions about the people we toss aside.

With that being said, you also need to be careful about keeping people who do not deserve to be kept. There are people who will not respect your boundaries. Hateful, mean-spirited, disrespectful, blatantly hurtful, and abusive people have no place in your life or in your children's lives. As Jen Hatmaker said in her book *For the Love*, "Allowing someone to wound you repeatedly is not a kindness." Think of this in terms of barriers. Imagine you have an open gate that leads right to you. Out from that, there is a locked gate that requires a key (permission) to get through, and even farther out there is a wall with no gate (no access). Depending on their level of toxicity, you get to decide where to allow the people in your life. Inside the open gate, there should be no toxic people. Take advice from Rumi, who said, "Set your life on fire and seek those who fan your flames." Your home and your inner circle should only be filled with flame fanners—people who love you well, treat you with respect, and see your value.

Just outside the locked gate are people who you love and who love you, but they sometimes leave you with negative emotions. They may be critical, demanding, or hurtful at times. These people may leave you feeling emotionally drained with too much exposure, but you can handle them in small increments. Inform these people of your boundary and keep them outside the gate until the point in which they earn a key (if that time ever comes). For example, you might need to say, "I won't allow you to keep criticizing my parenting choices. I'm doing what I think is right for my family. I would love to talk to you, but you have to keep your criticism to yourself." This will probably be a really uncomfortable conversation that takes no small amount of courage, but it's a necessary step. Some people did not grow up with healthy boundaries and may not think they are doing any harm. Do them the courtesy of informing them why they are locked outside the gate, and let them know how to earn a key.

Behind the gateless wall are the abusers and the ones who refuse to respect your boundaries. You do not have to feel guilt for putting these people outside the wall. You have the right to protect your family and your well-being.

The Mud Doesn't Get Glovey

My husband tells me, "When you throw a white glove in the mud, the glove gets muddy; the mud doesn't get white." I wasn't sure if he made that up himself or if he read it somewhere, so I entered the quote into my search bar. What I found was a poem by Dean Wood called "The Mud Won't Get Glovey." I like the sound of that better (sorry, Hubby!), but it means the same thing. Negativity can rub off on you. If you have to spend time with toxic people, your glove may get muddy. Your mood may sour or you may start to feel irritable, sad, or hurt. Be aware of how they have affected you and take care not to carry your muddied glove into your home. Our interactions with toxic people can easily affect our interactions with our children and loved ones if we aren't mindful.

In their book *Boundaries,* Drs. Henry Cloud and John Townsend say, "One sure sign of boundary problems is when your relationship with one person has the power to affect your relationship with others. You are giving one person way too much power in your life." I've experienced this truth in my personal life, and, in fact, it used to happen to me quite frequently. After phone conversations with a certain person left me feeling inadequate, shamed, and angry, I would carry my bad mood with me long after we'd hung up the phone. My emotions would be heightened for the rest of the day, and I would be irritable or withdrawn. I had a hard time letting those hurt feelings go. My muddied glove would end up leaving stains throughout the whole house, and yet the person on the other end of the line never did get "glovey." That person never understood how their words cut me, and even when I said as much, my words were shrugged off as though I was being overly sensitive. So, I had to create a strong boundary and put that person outside of my locked gate. That means that conversations are limited, and at the first sign of criticism or judgment, I end the conversation. I don't sit and listen to it anymore.

My Step-by-Step Guide for Dealing with Toxic People

1. Assess the level of toxicity in the relationship. Is the person intentionally hurtful, or is it simply a personality difference that makes the relationship difficult? Someone can be loved through a personality difference. Intentionally hurtful people have to go. To determine the level of toxicity, ask yourself the following questions:

Does this person love me?

Does this person have my best interests at heart?

Does this person respect me?

How do I usually feel after spending time with this person?

What bugs me about this person?

Does this person respect my boundaries?

2. Determine what barrier to put them behind depending on their level of toxicity. Love the ones you can love. Leave the ones you must leave. Be on the lookout for the sneaky ones, like that friend who is always complaining about her partner or children, Negative Nancy who sees the bad in everything, and those friends who are constantly involved in drama. Their issues may not be *about* you, but they still *affect* you.

3. State your boundaries clearly to those who need to hear them. If given the chance, maybe they will change how they treat you or behave around you. Many toxic people do not realize they are toxic. Upon hearing your boundaries, they may gain a whole new respect for you. At least by stating your boundaries clearly, you know who is willing to respect them and who isn't. It makes the decision to keep people behind your gateless wall easier to make.

4.　Say no to the guilt. If there is someone you have to cut out of your life, then you have not made that decision lightly. You've put them through the toxicity test and you've given them a chance to honor your boundaries. There is nothing more you can do, so don't feel guilt for saying good-bye. In the end, some people just do not belong in our lives. We have to make those decisions very carefully, but then we have to *honor ourselves* enough to stick to our decision and move on.

Toxic Habits

The greatest source of toxicity in your life may not be a person but one of your own habits. Like toxic people, we must also apply boundaries to ourselves so that bad habits don't pollute our happiness.

Let's take a look at some common toxic habits.

Yelling

Motherhood often brings us face-to-face with our tempers. Just underneath the surface of the white-hot anger and even rage that bubbles up inside us is fear, anxiety, or frustration. Sometimes it catches us off guard and scares us, and then it always causes deep, aching guilt. The explosive anger and yelling that ensue have a definite toxic effect on our relationships with our children and on our own health.

A University of Pittsburgh study found that yelling at children has damaging effects similar to physical discipline. That's sobering news. Their study concluded that yelling actually reinforces bad behavior and increases depression in children. And all those stress hormones aren't good for moms, either.

Break the habit: There are several helpful ways to approach this problem. By learning about age-appropriate development in children, you will learn when you are expecting too much and when you may not be expecting quite enough. Knowing what they are capable of at their particular stage reduces stress and gives you a clearer picture of how to parent. In addition, learning to manage your anger triggers, lower your stress, and take better care of yourself will help you be a calmer, happier parent.

Complaining

If you've ever been around someone who is a complainer, you know how draining it is. Yet, it's an easy trap to fall into because our brains *make it easy.* Complaining actually rewires our brain to see the world negatively and, because neurons that fire together wire together, our brains end up running down that same familiar path of complaints over and over again. It's an ugly cycle that is toxic not only for your brain but also for the brains of your family members. Complaining is a bit like secondhand smoke. It'll have a negative effect on anyone who is close enough to you to breathe it in. Of course, another downside to complaining is that your children will model your behavior. Suddenly you'll have a house full of complaining children, and that's no fun for anyone.

Break the habit: Spend a full day noticing how many times you complain. It might be an eye-opener! Lots of times, we don't even realize we complain so much, but when we bring our awareness to it, we can stop the habit. If you notice that you often complain about something in particular, then set a goal to change that one thing. Looking for real solutions is more effective than simply voicing displeasure.

Changing your language is also helpful in beating the complaining habit. Look for positive ways to state what you want rather than negative ways of stating what you don't. For example, "Nobody ever picks up after themselves around here," isn't as likely to spur action as, "Hey, I'd like you to pick up that trash and throw it away, and then straighten up your room. Thank you for being helpful!" Not only will you get more accomplished, but you'll feel happier, too.

Finally, it's impossible to complain and be grateful at the same time, so whenever you are getting ready to voice a complaint, try to pause and think of something you're grateful for. As Rita Schiano said, "Talking about our problems is our greatest addiction. Break the habit. Talk about your joys."

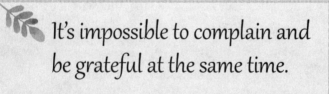

It's impossible to complain and be grateful at the same time.

Spending Too Much Time on Our Phones

I saw a quote from Kim Uliana that said, "Your phone won't feel bad if you don't pay attention to it. It won't care if you haven't played with it in a while. It won't mind if you don't hold it. Your cell phone will be small forever; your children will not." Gut punch, right?

I try hard to be mindful about my phone and social media usage, but like so many of us, sometimes I get caught up in it. Sometimes my work requires me to be connected more than I care to be. And frankly, sometimes I zone out while I aimlessly scroll. I don't want to add to your guilt; we all deal with enough of that! This isn't about shaming moms for using our phones. This is simply about *mindful usage.*

Connecting with friends on social media, playing an occasional game, and reading informative and inspirational pieces can add happiness to our lives. There are some friends and pages that I follow whose status updates and shares brighten my day. I've read articles that have seriously made me a better wife and mother. However, we have to be honest with ourselves about how lost we get in our devices so that we can both model good boundary setting for our children and make sure we aren't missing out on the best moments of our lives.

I see two issues with frequent phone use. One is that we cannot straddle two worlds. I am either engaged online or I am engaged in real life. I'm either seeing the status updates of my friends and acquaintances, or I'm seeing the people right in front of me. The second problem is that our social media newsfeeds and the online content we are subjected to can be a real drag. The online world is filled with endless debates, negative articles, and bad news. This can have an unpleasant effect on the psyche.

Break the habit: Do you see a lot of drama in your newsfeed? Is there a friend or family member whose posts make you feel blah? Are you inundated with articles and messages from pages you've followed that are filled with whining and complaining, or whose messages do not align with the direction in which you want your life to go? Block out a stretch of time to clean up your Facebook and other social media accounts. In Facebook, you can go to your settings and click on newsfeed preferences. This allows you to control what you see. Here, you can unfollow Negative Nancy, Complaining Carol, Political Paula, and anyone else who gives you negative vibes. You don't have to unfriend them (although you can), but you can unfollow them and they won't even know. Also, clean up the pages you are following. If they aren't inspirational or adding some value to your life, ditch them. Create a newsfeed of Zen and happiness.

After you have cleaned up your accounts, create boundaries around your phone use by declaring certain times of day to be phone-free. Put it away while you eat dinner with your family. Don't have it near you during family movies, games, or story time. I'm hoping that if I don't make my kids compete with my phone for my attention now, they won't make me compete with their phones when they're older. One can hope, right?

Sacrificing Sleep

I write this to myself as much as I am writing it to you. I'm so bad at this one! I love the chill time I get when my kids go to bed. The trouble is that my kids are older now and they go to bed later. I usually shower after they go to bed, and by the time all is said and done, it's close to 11:00 p.m. when I settle down for the night. I usually wrap up work for the day at around eleven thirty and then, finally, I'll put on an audiobook or watch a Netflix show with my husband. Often, it's 1:00 or 2:00 a.m. before I turn everything off. I'm only logging about five hours of sleep per night.

A lot of mamas admit to sacrificing sleep for quiet alone time.

I've shared several posts about this subject on my parenting page on Facebook, and they're some of the most popular posts because they resonate with so many moms. Our psyches need that time when we aren't being poked, jumped on, sat on, tugged at, yelled for, or talked to. In my *mind*, I'd rather lose a couple of hours of sleep than give up my sacred alone time.

Unfortunately, my body disagrees with my mind, and so does yours. Sleep is crucial to our overall health and well-being. Studies have shown that those who sleep fewer than six hours per night (ahem) are 12 percent more likely to die prematurely. Sleep is essential for our immune systems, memory, cell repair, and even steady blood sugar levels. Getting fewer than seven or eight hours per night leads to increased risk of diabetes, heart disease, and obesity. This is such bad news.

Break the habit: Here's my plan, and I hope you'll consider joining me. I'm going to allow myself three nights a week to stay up late and do what I want, but I'll go to bed early the other four nights. This isn't as good as getting optimal sleep seven nights a week, but I'm trying to be realistic. When breaking hard habits, sometimes we just have to take baby steps. This is a baby step habit for me, but maybe you'll choose to get to bed early every night. Either way, here's to a good night's sleep for our health and happiness!

Comparisons

I saw her step out of her shiny clean SUV in pumps. Her bleached-blond (yet somehow not frizzy or broken) hair caught the wind as she closed her car door and strutted into the school building with her kid. She had on full makeup at 7:45 a.m., and her daughter looked like she'd had a makeover that very morning, all bright and shiny and matching. I watched my own kid walk to the door, his hair sticking up in the back, dragging his backpack like a ball and chain. A quick glance in the mirror reflected dark circles that I hadn't yet put concealer on, and a big zit on my chin. Let's not even discuss my grungy outfit. Clearly, she was winning and I was losing.

I know that comparison is the thief of joy and all that, yet it's so hard not to do, isn't it? When the other first graders were reading way ahead of mine, I compared. When my husband lost thirty pounds and I lost just one doing the same exercise program, I compared. When my author friend hit the *New York Times* bestseller list, I compared. You get the picture. The thing is, we tend to compare our worst to everyone else's best, which makes it a really unfair comparison. This toxic habit will destroy your self-confidence and make a huge dent in your level of happiness, so it's best to nip it in the bud.

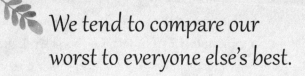

We tend to compare our
worst to everyone else's best.

Break the habit: According to psychologists Adam Galinsky and Maurice Schweitzer, social comparison is an innate human tendency. It's one way we determine our level of happiness. We aren't wrong or bad for comparing ourselves to others, but it can become a destructive habit, particularly when we spend a lot of time in negative comparisons. The next time you find yourself comparing your life to someone else's, remind yourself to look more objectively. What might that person have gone through to get where she is? Is she likely dealing with pain, suffering, or difficulty in her life that you are unaware of? Most people are. Then wish her well and whisper a word of gratitude for your life.

Strategy: Creating Boundaries

Whether you are dealing with a toxic person or a toxic habit, creating boundaries is key to ditching the problem and finding more happiness. We've already discussed at length how to create boundaries with toxic people, and each "break the habit" section requires us to set boundaries with ourselves. Some toxic habits also necessitate setting boundaries on others, particularly if they are part of your toxic habit, such as excessive drinking or gossiping.

Setting boundaries can be uncomfortable and even downright scary. You may fear that people won't like you, will see you as being mean, or will be disappointed in you. Setting boundaries on your own behavior can also be difficult as there is no one to answer to but you! However, boundaries are essential to rid your life of the toxicity that is impeding your happiness.

Happiness Habit

It is said that we are the average of the five people we hang out with most. Do you have a toxic person in your five? Think of the most cheerful friend you have. How often do you hang out? If you don't have a cheerful friend, then, girl, it's time to get new friends! Surround yourself with happy people and you'll find that you're happier, too.

Journal Prompts

1. Name one toxic habit that you need to ditch. What boundary can you set?

2. List three benefits you'll receive by ditching that toxic habit.

3. Name the five people you spend the most time with. Are they happy, positive people?

4. What is your biggest fear about setting boundaries?

5. How can you attract more happy people into your life? Where might you find them?

Chapter Eight

Mind-set Matters

Always remember, your focus determines your reality.
—Qui-Gon Jinn

The morning sun peeked through the shades of my bedroom window, casting alternating slivers of light and dark onto the floor. I had awoken only moments before to a very familiar sound, and I watched the sunbeams dancing on my rug as I waited for him to appear. He bounded in and leaped onto my bed. "Good morning, Mommy," he said cheerfully, adding a heart-tugging "I love you!" He lay down beside me and wrapped one arm around my waist. I placed my arm under his head as I always did and wrapped him up in both arms. We call this "the snuggle-bunny hug." In that moment, I felt so much gratitude for that boy and his love, for that sunny morning, and for the chance of another day with my family. It was pure joy.

I was once again jerked from my much-needed sleep by the sound of a kid getting out of bed too soon. I blinked into the bright rays assaulting my eyes. How could it possibly be morning already? I stared grumpily at the beams of light strewn across my floor and made a mental note to get room-darkening curtains. Maybe putting them over his window as well would keep him in bed longer. He came running into my room, jumping on the bed and jarring me from my comfortable position. "Good morning, Mommy!" he said too loudly, and I shot him a look of irritation. He didn't seem to notice. "I love you," he said, and he nestled in beside me. *If you loved me, you'd let me sleep*, I thought. I put my arms around him and sighed. Another busy day with not enough hours or energy. I felt so frustrated.

Which one is true? The same thing happened in both stories; the only difference was my mind-set. Story one demonstrated a positive mind-set, whereas the other showed a negative one. It was my choice to feel either gratitude or frustration when my son jumped onto my bed. I had the power to choose either story I wanted. On that particular morning, I chose gratitude, but there have certainly been days that I chose frustration, too. We always have a choice in how we look at the days we are given. We can choose to let our days rule us, or we can consciously choose to rule our days. We can let our situation determine our moods and levels of happiness, or we can determine to be positive and find joy regardless of the situation, or to at least not get stuck in despair.

Actively Choosing Joy

Every day, my line of work brings me in contact with many articles on parenting and motherhood, and every day I read headlines that declare how bad we have it. Moms are crying out. We want to feel validated, heard, and cared for. We want to feel less alone, and so we gather online to commiserate about the difficulties of motherhood. I understand the need to feel like you are not alone in your struggles. It can feel really good to hear someone else say, "Yes! It is so hard for me, too!" We shouldn't keep silent when we are having a hard time, and I'm happy that we feel like we can collectively exhale and admit our problems, but I worry about how this could quickly become a negativity trap.

There's a difference between acknowledging that there are dark days and deciding to dwell in the darkness. Saying "Yes, this can be difficult, but I've got this" is profoundly different from being stuck in "Ugh, this is so hard. I can't even." I also question if social media is the right place to reach out for help. When I speak one-on-one with someone I trust, I feel heard. I can admit my frustration to my friend and perhaps she will admit hers, and then the conversation naturally turns. We don't dwell there in that frustration. However, in the online world, comments heap upon comments, dozens or even hundreds of mothers join in to nod their heads, and in that environment, a passing frustration becomes something more. This inevitably affects the narrative in our minds.

This isn't an easy issue to write about. There are so many gray areas. Our collective mental health is suffering for a myriad of reasons, and I don't pretend to have answers. What I can attest to is that focusing on hardships without working toward a solution tends to make them more emotionally charged rather than alleviating the stress. Studies show that complaining usually leads to more complaining, and it's easy to get caught up in such a negative cycle that you miss the joy in your days. I know—I've been there.

Mind-set matters. While it may feel temporarily good to connect with other moms on the difficult aspects of mothering, we have to ask ourselves what it's doing to our mind-set. Does it do us good to vent, or does it build on negative feelings? I wonder how much our happiness would increase if we took as much time to nourish our positive feelings and to dwell in the feelings of joy for as long as we dwell in the frustrations. Moms, we have to guard our minds. I believe it's as simple and as difficult as that. We have to make conscious choices on the thoughts we allow to run through it and on what we allow in. For me, that means scrolling past those "this is so hard" posts and focusing my mind on the joys of motherhood.

This is not a Pollyannaish approach. I'm not suggesting at all that we discount the truths that motherhood can be taxing. I fully acknowledge that parenthood brings exhaustion, worry, fear, sleepless nights, hurt feelings, broken hearts, messes everywhere, anxiety, and more. But it also brings laughter, smiles, hugs, tiny hands in mine, arms around my neck, the sweet rhythmic breathing of a child sleeping next to me, mornings that start with "good morning, Mommy," love notes, stick people drawings, sticky kisses, healing, and love. So much love. My happiness (and yours) is largely dependent on which of those I choose to focus on. It doesn't have to be easy or perfect to be really, really good.

We have a choice as to how we perceive our motherhood experience. Let's not set ourselves up to dwell on the difficulties but to dwell on the joys. Here are three tips for greater happiness.

1. **Value what you do.** So much of my own frustrations as a mom of little ones came from feeling undervalued. Because it takes so much time and nurturance for the seeds we are planting to grow and bear fruit, it often feels like we aren't getting much accomplished each day, even after all our efforts. We pour everything into our kids, and sometimes all we get in return is another tantrum. I know that it can feel like a thankless job, but what you are doing each day is the most important work there is.

2. **Guard your mind and your mouth.** Is what you're reading or watching each day encouraging you or is it discouraging you? Again, it's about making conscious choices. Determine what kind of attitude you want to have and what kind of mom you want to be. Whatever isn't leading you toward that, let it go. Likewise, watch the language you use and in whom you confide. This *isn't* about holding in your frustrations but letting them out and then moving through. Will it really help to throw a comment into the pile in a moms' group, or would it be wiser to talk to your partner, friend, mom, or maybe a counselor? Make wise choices that move you forward.

3. **Move from complaining to problem solving.** If you find yourself discussing with your partner or friend how difficult motherhood is, move to find a solution so that you don't stay in that negative space. If you're struggling because you are sleep deprived, brainstorm ways to get more rest. If feeling

overwhelmed is the problem, work together to lighten the load. Don't remain stuck. There is too much beauty to be seen in your days, dear Mama.

Strategy: Develop a Growth Mind-set

Growth mind-set has become a buzzword in recent years. It is talked about a lot in education and is the culmination of the research by Dr. Carol Dweck. She coined the terms *fixed mind-set* and *growth mind-set* to describe the underlying beliefs people have about learning. She noted that students who believe they can get smarter and understand that effort make them stronger put in more time and effort and achieve more. On the other hand, students with a fixed mind-set feel stuck. They believe that you are either good at something or you're not. A person with a fixed mind-set believes that abilities and attributes are fixed and unchanged, whereas someone with a growth mind-set believes these can be developed and improved.

Why is this important for moms? Surely no one besides a student undergoes more growth than a mother during her children's childhoods. Only with a growth mind-set can we believe in our abilities to learn and improve at parenting, and having that belief in ourselves and our abilities will affect how happy and confident we feel doing it. Mistakes don't choke us when we have a growth mind-set. Instead, they highlight where we need to improve and, believing that we have the ability to change, we get about the business of improving it.

Many moms, though, believe they are either good at being a mom or just weren't cut out for it. They think they're either a natural at it or not. This is a fixed mind-set in parenting, and it stifles our growth and limits our potential. If we feel stuck in our parenting, we aren't likely to put in the effort toward making positive changes when we need to, and that can leave us trapped in unhealthy or unhelpful patterns. Take the limitations off yourself by:

- Becoming aware of your strengths and weaknesses

- Using positive self-talk

- Viewing mistakes as opportunities to learn

- Not staying stuck in regret or shame

A growth mind-set is a positive mind-set. It means that, even if today was hard, you feel hope for tomorrow. You may visit despair, anger, frustration, exasperation, and sadness, but you don't stay there. You believe in yourself and in your ability to overcome obstacles, figure out challenges, try new things, and succeed as a mom. That's a pretty great gift to give yourself and your children.

> *The view you adopt of yourself profoundly*
> *affects the way you live your life.*
> —Carol Dweck

Happiness Habit

Work on building your resilience. Practice bouncing back quickly from mistakes and upsets and on owning your mood and mind-set. Here are five steps to building resilience. Take one challenging situation you're currently facing and work through these steps.

1. **Practice optimism.** Write down a few positive thoughts now.

_____

_____

_____

2. **Reframe the problem.** Rather than looking at it negatively, see if you can reframe it in a positive way. For example, what we call "the terrible twos," the Danes call "the boundary stage." Do you see how just the language changes the emotional reaction you have and therefore the action you are likely to take? Reframe a problem you are dealing with now.

_____

_____

_____

3. **Develop a growth mind-set** and a belief in yourself as a mom. Self-esteem plays an important role in coping with stress. Write down two things you do well in parenting.

_____

_____

_____

4. **Develop your problem-solving skills.** When you encounter a problem, get to work on fixing it rather than lamenting about it. Think of a problem you are currently dealing with and jot down two possible solutions.

_____

_____

_____

5. **Practice consistent self-care.** Write down one way to nurture yourself today.

_____

_____

_____

Journal Prompts

1. Do you feel you have a fixed mind-set or a growth mind-set?

2. Write down three things that trigger bad moods for you.

3. Write down three things that improve your mood.

4. Name one person you will call or confide in about your troubles.

5. List three ways to avoid getting stuck in despair.

Chapter Nine

Letting Go of Guilt

It's shocking, isn't it? Motherhood.

The way it stretches not only your body but your mind and spirit, too. It stretches your ideas, your judgments, your dreams, and your fears. It takes your ego and throws it high into the air, then catches it and slams it down onto the ground hard. It forces you to confront the worst parts of yourself, sometimes by staring down into fierce little eyes that mirror your own determination or rage.

Motherhood isn't just about raising children. Motherhood is where you, yourself, are raised up to your highest potential, if you're open to it; if you listen.

You know this is big. You understand how high the calling of motherhood is, and it's beautiful and joyous and amazing. And it's heavy. And every day you show up one more time and try. That takes courage.

No one tells you how brave it is to show up every single day when so very much is at stake. Sometimes you might have to crawl out of bed or off the floor and straighten those shoulders up, put on your best fake smile, and dust off yesterday's perceived failures, but you do it. Day after day.

Your mama heart wants so, so much to get this right. You love those babies so much it hurts, and when you slip up, when you snap at one of them, when you yell after promising not to yell anymore, when you feel like you have let them down, guilt and regret pool in your chest and it burns your throat.

The tears fall behind the bathroom door again, and your inner bully is relentless. She tears into you when you lay your head on your pillow after the kids are finally asleep, and no rest comes.

When you get a negative call from school or catch your pre-schooler telling lies or your toddler bites her friend, you wonder where you went wrong and if they're going to turn out okay despite your mistakes and shortcomings. When your teen slams the door in your face or the night's homework battle turns into full-on war and you're dripping tears on the math worksheet you're checking, I know you feel like a failure.

Here's what you need to know, Mama. The rest of us have cried in our bathrooms, too. Every other mother there ever was has felt those feelings of guilt and has worried if they were getting it completely wrong at one time or another, so please don't believe that the rest of us are getting this motherhood thing right every day while you're struggling to find your way.

We are all trying to find our way. None of us is perfect. Not one.

Guilt weighs heavy on the hearts of so many mothers. It nestles in, an unwelcomed guest, and makes a home inside our hearts, causing it to sink with the pressure of its weight. We are juggling an

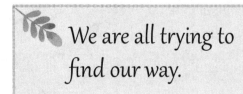

We are all trying to find our way.

impossible amount of responsibilities and often feeling unsure if we have given enough, even though at the end of the day there is absolutely nothing left to give. We go to bed completely spent and wonder where our currency went. Did I love enough today? Did I spend enough time with each child? Did I listen to my partner? Did I let down that friend? So many "shoulds" run rampant through our tired minds, stealing peace and eroding happiness. I should have done this, or I shouldn't have done that. We promise to do better tomorrow with all of our very best intentions. Then tomorrow comes with the same flurry of responsibilities that yesterday had, and our best never feels quite good enough.

In a small sampling of 125 mothers that I surveyed on social media, an overwhelming 82 percent admitted to struggling with mom guilt. While it was in no way a peer-reviewed scientific study, it's certainly sobering evidence that few mothers seem to be able to escape guilt entirely. Working moms, stay-at-home moms, single moms, married moms—all of us feel its grip sometimes. Do you know what, Mama? If you didn't care so much, it wouldn't bother you. The fact that you do experience guilt speaks volumes about the love you have for your children and your desire to mother them well. Still, it can become a poison, so we need to talk about this heavy guilt that you're carrying.

You feel guilty because you yelled.

You feel guilty because they're not in bed yet.

You feel guilty for having another baby.

Guilt for not having another baby.

Guilt for not breastfeeding at all or for long enough or maybe for too long (according to other people).

Guilt for feeding them mac and cheese again or for having a picky eater.

Guilt for sleep training.

Guilt for co-sleeping.

Guilt for getting angry.

You may even feel guilt for feeling guilty instead of being a happier mom! There are a million different reasons why mothers feel guilty, but there's one good reason to stop wallowing in the muck of guilt.

It's not helping you.

Just to be clear, not *all* guilt is bad. It comes in varying degrees of severity and toxicity. Sometimes it is specific and appropriate and points to a need for action. An example is perhaps you yelled at your children or said something hurtful to your partner. The guilt you feel then is a warning sign that you crossed a boundary and need to make amends and work toward better reactions in the future.

At other times, though, guilt is generalized or inappropriate. For example, you may feel guilty for co-sleeping with your child after talking with a mom who has an independent sleeper. Even though there is nothing wrong with your behavior and co-sleeping suits you just fine, guilt seeps in because you begin to compare your situation to someone else's and question your choices.

In other words, guilt can be a catalyst for positive change or a disease that eats away at your self-worth and actually hinders your ability to do better. Your conscience is an important guide; it makes you human and points you back to your values. Yet allowing guilt to become excessive and chronic rather than recognizing whether it is appropriate or inappropriate and handling it accordingly is a dangerous trap.

Sure, guilt in small doses helps keep us in check, but most of us are *overdosing* on guilt, and this actually keeps us from moving forward. Studies have found that concentration, productivity, creativity, and efficiency go way down when you're stuck in guilt. As I've studied child development over the years, I have learned that a child who is in emotional distress cannot be his best self, and yet I, too, often forget that the same is true for me. Unchecked guilt *is* emotional distress and can lead to anxiety, depression, and a host of other problems. That heavy load is fogging up your brain, making it difficult to think straight. It's giving the bully in your head free rein. That negative self-talk is sucking out your happiness and replacing it with anxiety. It's keeping you from enjoying your life.

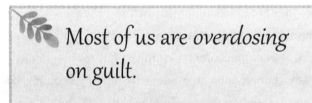

Most of us are *overdosing* on guilt.

We all make choices we wish we could change. I've condemned myself for months over a ten-second mistake but never praised myself for months over a small achievement. I tend to be very hard on myself, and that's a sentiment too many mothers can relate to. You can only hear so many "you're screwing this up" messages before you start believing that you're a screwup, and those messages are everywhere these days, aren't they?

In one single day, I came across several headlines that suggested, even if ever so kindly, that I was parenting wrong. One headline read, ARE YOU OVER-PARENTING? It went on to tell me all of the ways my children would fail at life if I parented too much, and I started questioning myself. Am I over-parenting? How exactly does one *parent too much*? I packed my eleven-year-old's lunch for him. Is he doomed? Have I crippled him for life because I took his ukulele to school when he forgot it at home? Silly questions seem valid when you're suddenly gripped with guilt.

The next headline that got my attention alluded to a person being damaged for life because of one sentence her mother uttered when she was a child. Scarred for life over one sentence. I started racking my brain, wondering if I'd ever said anything that could have potentially scarred my kid for life. The weight of that thought was unbearable. What the author of the article described as scarring wasn't something I thought could have had such a negative impact over a lifetime, so it left me wondering if I had casually said something in passing that my child took the wrong way. Had words I meant to be constructive criticism pierced his soul? Was it really so easy to break someone? Those were frightening thoughts.

Later that day, I discovered that I was supposed to attend a presentation by my third grader, even though he'd told me the day before that parents weren't supposed to come. Still, all the other moms attended, and I felt guilty that I had missed it. By the end of the night, after I'd needed to skip my living room date with my husband and tell my kids I couldn't play because I had to work late to meet a deadline, I was in full guilt mode, feeling like a total screwup. I recognized I was carrying a heavy load and unpacked it, showing myself a bit of grace along the way. I am trying really hard over here. I know you are, too.

So can I tell you right now that you are not a screwup? No matter how many times you have made the same mistake, this is a new day and anything is possible. Can I remind you of all the times you've kissed the hurt places, sat up with a sick child through the night, and rocked a crying baby even though your eyes and your heart were heavy? Can I point out all the times you have fed your kids first to make sure they had their fill before you ate, passed up what you wanted so you could buy things for your child, loitered outside in the halls of the school to make sure your kid was going to be okay, and braved through tough conversations so your child would be informed and empowered? Can I emphasize how you've listened to your child spread fears and dreams before you, comforted an upset baby, and encouraged a beating heart?

If there are a million reasons for you to feel guilty, then there are also a million reasons for you to feel like an amazing mother. I do not believe that your kids are holding your mistakes against you, especially your young ones. They love you and, more than anything, they just want to see you happy. You're not a screwup to them. You are their whole world. Even older children forgive easily with a heartfelt apology and proven sincerity.

So let it go, Mama. Apologize if you need to and change your behavior if that's required. Then just let it go. **Guilt stops by to teach us a lesson, but we invite it in for tea and give it a place in our bed.** Listen to what it's telling you and then let it wash away like the dirt from the day and get on with living and loving. Just don't hold on to it for dear life, because there are so many better things worth holding on to.

How to Let It Go

Letting go of guilt is really a simple process. It only requires us to do something that we might not be so used to doing well—loving and forgiving ourselves.

The first step to letting it go is to determine what your guilt is telling you. Remember that it is only supposed to be a visitor, not a permanent resident in your mind. Is the guilt attached to a judgment of yourself or to someone else's judgment of you? Is it appropriate? Is there a need for you to make amends or change your behavior?

If the answer is yes, that your guilt is appropriate and calls for action, then turn your guilt into fuel for making the change happen. Here are the steps for releasing appropriate guilt:

1. **Apologize to whomever you hurt, if necessary.** Understand that your guilt is a powerful sign of empathy. It means you are a *good* and caring person. You feel guilty because you want to do the right thing. By apologizing, you are both showing respect to the one you wronged and proving your willingness to change. Sincere apologies often help you release the guilt while helping the other person release anger.

2. **Think about why you behaved in such a way that caused someone harm or didn't align with your values.** Was a personal boundary crossed? Do you need stronger boundaries, then? Are your needs not being met? When you get to the root of what caused your behavior, you can determine how to correct it. This is the way to forgiveness and healing. Only by making a change in your behavior can you prevent

future damage to the relationship and the heart of the person you hurt.

3. **Create a plan of action that leads to a positive goal.** Focus on achieving what you want rather than stopping what you don't want. For example, rather than making a goal "not to yell," instead make a goal to "take mindful breaths when anger arises." Working toward a positive goal is often more fruitful than fighting against a negative behavior.

If, on the other hand, the answer is no, your guilt is not appropriate and is arising from someone else's judgment of you, then understand that this is not your burden to carry and let it go. In cognitive theory, thoughts cause emotions, so if you change your thoughts, your emotions change as well. By intentionally thinking positive, self-compassionate thoughts, you will move out of guilt and into positive emotions. So instead of "I should go back to work and contribute more to my family" or "I should quit my job and stay home with my baby," think, "I'm doing the best I can today, and we are doing just fine."

You have to stop being so hard on yourself. You have to extend to yourself the same love and tenderness and grace that you try to extend to your children because as much as they need it, you need it, too.

And do you want to know a little secret? The more you treat yourself with gentleness, the more gentleness you can show others.

Make it your goal to shine a spotlight on your own goodness, successes, triumphs, and bravery, and tonight, when you finally climb underneath the covers, don't replay your mistakes in your mind.

Replay how much you loved. Give yourself a little grace. Perhaps that's the bravest thing of all.

Strategy: Self-Acceptance, Self-Forgiveness, and Responsibility

The ability to forgive yourself is essential for your emotional well-being. However, as with all things, it can be overused. If we practice self-forgiveness without taking responsibility for our actions, then we may not have the motivation to change our behavior. However, if we are good at taking responsibility, making amends, and changing behavior but we do not practice self-forgiveness, then we may spiral into shame. Therefore, there needs to be a healthy balance of both taking responsibility when necessary (for appropriate guilt) and self-forgiveness.

If guilt acknowledges the bad aspects of ourselves and our behavior, then self-forgiveness acknowledges our good aspects and ability to change. Forgiveness alone doesn't motivate better behavior, but neither does guilt alone. It is both acknowledging your wrongdoing and acknowledging your ability to improve that allow you to make positive changes. Once you have sought forgiveness from the one you have wronged, self-forgiveness is a necessary step toward releasing yourself from guilt and helping you take the next step.

If your guilt is not appropriate in the first place, then there is no need to forgive yourself, for you haven't done anything wrong. What you need in this case is self-acceptance. Many mamas fail to see their strengths and accomplishments but are good at highlighting their failures and weaknesses. No one judges us more than we judge ourselves, and in the current culture, that's saying something! If the goal is to give your child a happy mom, then self-acceptance must be part of the plan. I believe one of the ideas that blocks us from self-acceptance is the idea that we must approve of whatever we accept. It feels like accepting ourselves for the things we feel we've done wrong is like saying what we did is okay. That's not true! Accepting ourselves in spite of our mistakes is an admittance that, even with our flaws, imperfections, and wrongdoings, we are still worthy of love. Show yourself some love, dear one.

Happiness Habit

In this powerful exercise, I want you to write down everything you can think of that you need to forgive yourself for. After you've written them down, read them aloud, beginning with, "I forgive myself for . . ." Come back and repeat this exercise each and every day until you feel the weight begin to lift off your heart.

Journal Prompts

1. What would your teenage self think about you now?

2. Finish the sentence, "I love myself because . . ."

3. What is your best personality trait and why?

4. What three words would your best friend use to describe you?

5. What would you say to your child who is stuck in guilt about a mistake he or she made? Why shouldn't you say the same to yourself?

Chapter Ten

Mental Overload

I sometimes think that if I could tip my head to the side and shake it a bit so that everything swirling around inside my brain would fall out onto the floor, all my thoughts would come rushing out like the herd of rhinos in *Jumanji* and terrorize the town. That's sort of what they all feel like stomping around in my head. On the other hand, if my husband were to do the same, I imagine a tiny, happy wisp of smoke floating out and rising to the clouds.

I'm not saying his head is empty, so don't take that the wrong way! My husband is an incredibly intelligent, considerate, loving companion and an involved, devoted father who deserves tons of credit. It just seems to me that he is capable of closing a metaphorical window in his mind before opening up a new one; therefore, whatever would fall out of his brain would just be the contents of one window—a wisp in comparison to my jumbled rhino herd. On the other hand, my brain looks remarkably similar to my laptop. There are countless windows open, and they're all running simultaneously.

Mark Gungor, chief executive officer of Laugh Your Way America, explains the differences between men's and women's brains like this. "Men's brains are made up of little boxes, and we have a box for everything. . . . The rule is: the boxes do not touch. . . . Women's brains are made up of a big ball of wire, and everything is connected to everything." When he says this in his speech, the audience erupts with laughter. It's funny, but it also sounds familiar, right?

My husband, Eric, jokingly recounts one particular day when the reality of my mental workload was abundantly clear. He came home to find a cold pizza sitting on top of the stove, but the oven was still on. The pizza had been cooked, so that's a win. I just forgot to turn the oven off. After he turned off the oven, he went downstairs to the laundry room to check if my clothes needed to be brought up. He's always on top of the laundry and is helping me get it done. Isn't that sexy? He found that I'd thrown a load into the washer and poured in the detergent but never started the machine. He pressed the start button and came back upstairs. When he entered my office space, he found me fighting with my laptop. "Arrgh! I cannot get this thing to charge. I have no idea what is wrong with this stupid hunk of junk!" "Here, I'll take a look," he offered. I stormed out to the kitchen to grab a glass of water and when I came back in, he exclaimed, "I fixed it!" He laughed. "It had come unplugged from the wall." Of course it had.

Honestly, I have a lot of days like that. I forget things often because how is it *even possible* to keep up with everything? As great as Eric is, he just doesn't think about all the things I have to keep up with on a daily basis, like making sure all the bills are paid, checking the kids' backpacks and signing all the papers and planners and permission slips, keeping up with school projects and field-trip days and general happenings, my kids' basketball schedule and performing arts schedule, swimming lessons, packing and ordering lunches and checking their grades and graded papers, and keeping up with library books and such. I'm the one who writes down medicine schedules and gives them their vitamins. Tis I who sets my alarm at 3:00 a.m. to check fevers when they're sick, who takes them to the doctor, makes orthodontist appointments and eye doctor appointments (and shuttles them to and fro) and keeps up with immunization records. I'm the one who buys school supplies and poster boards for projects, who scours Michaels for diorama trees and plastic baby animals to go with it. I make sure my kids have clothes that actually fit and shoes that do, too.

The workload is never-ending. I'm in charge of arranging hangouts (they're too old and cool now to call them playdates) and buying birthday gifts for their friends. It's up to me to know who they're hanging out with and to get to know their friends' parents. I'm the one who keeps in contact with teachers and goes to the conferences. I wipe down the vents, dust the shades, and clean out the vacuum, though I admit it's always my husband who gets the dryer lint. I never remember the dryer lint until I've made a small quilt. He's great at running the vacuum and tidying up, but the small details of house cleaning apparently reside in my brain only. I have to keep up with our calendar and make sure there are no scheduling conflicts. If something were to happen to me, I wonder whether or not the kids would ever get haircuts or clipped fingernails. I imagine they'd look quite feral. I shudder to think of it.

It's not that he's incapable of keeping up with this stuff; it just doesn't seem to occur to him to do so. I know he'd gladly help out with the details if only I'd ask, but sometimes it eases my mind to take care of it myself. I suppose he thinks I have it all covered, and I kind of do, but it wears me out. And that's only the tip of the iceberg, because outside of thinking about all the things I actually have to do, my mind is constantly awhirl with the stuff I maybe should do or should have done in the past or with things I might possibly need to do in the future. I started thinking about how I could prepare them for the pressures of adolescence when they were toddlers. I think now about how to help them be good husbands and fathers one day, and they're not even teenagers yet. I think about how to prepare them for college and build resilience and a million other things that raising children entails.

My husband keeps up with a lot, too. I know he has a lot of pressures at work. He is very good at helping me with the household chores, as I said. He deals with our yard and fixes the things around the house that need repair. He puts together complicated toys and helps our boys build Lego sets. This is so not my forte. Still, it seems he has a beautifully uncomplicated mind, and I envy that immensely.

I also think that moms tend to take on more of the emotional load of a family. Not only do I feel responsible for my children's emotions, but I seem to just take them on as my own automatically. Have you heard the saying "A mother is only as happy as her saddest child"? It's true, isn't it? If one of my children is struggling emotionally, I feel the weight of it. It's almost impossible for me to feel happy unless everyone else in my family is feeling happy. I understand that negative emotions are part of the human experience, and I let my children feel them and try my best to help them process them. It's just that, through their emotional turmoil, I am feeling emotional turmoil, too, even if I don't let them see it. By contrast, Eric just nonchalantly says, "He'll work through it and be fine." He's capable of separating how he feels from how the children feel. I can't do that.

There is a giant backpack filled with the invisible work of parenthood, and mothers are often the ones breaking their backs lugging it around. It's not that fathers are doing something wrong or bad; it's just the way many moms' minds work. So, this chapter isn't about laying blame or lifting one parent above the other, not at all. It's just to say, "Yes, Mama, we feel it, too."

The mental workload of mothers is a happiness stealer for sure, so how can we combat this? Let's not kid ourselves. It's not going to go away. Our minds will always be filled to the brim, but there are strategies we can use to balance out feeling overwhelmed with being joyful. When we add more to our "happiness bucket" than is in our "overwhelm bucket," we can tip the scales in our favor and find more joy in the chaos of motherhood.

Strategy: Soul Deposits

The stars seemed to twinkle with delight against the clear, black sky. Each one was but a dot in the heavens, and yet each shone just as brightly as it could. I thought what a fitting representation of us they were, each only a speck but each with significant light. In the cool night air, the crickets chirped around us, the heavens sprawled out above us, and, as we lay there in silence marveling at the beauty before our eyes, my soul felt at rest.

My own soul seems to connect with the stars. It's almost as if they know each other—far-distance friends whispering *hello again*. I thought about how we were created by the same hands, and I marveled at the thought. Stretched beneath the splendor of the starry sky, my fingers intertwined with my son's, I had the acute realization that *this is life*. Not schedules and calendars. Not worries or newsfeeds. Those are merely time fillers. Life is beauty, splendor, awe, wonder, and, most of all, love.

On this gorgeous summer night, the four of us were stargazing in the hopes of seeing a shooting star. There was to be a meteor shower that night, and the boys' excitement was palpable as we gathered our pillows and blankets. Flashlight in hand, we made our way down the yard and climbed onto our trampoline. I laid one blanket down as a barrier between the cold, damp mesh and our backs, and then we fluffed our pillows and lay side by side underneath the stars. Soon, a bright streak flashed across the sky, and my kids excitedly proclaimed, "Did you see that!" We went on to see twenty-six more meteors that night, and it is forever engraved in my heart as one of the best, most awesome nights of my motherhood. Lying hand in hand with my children watching shooting stars travel across the sky was truly magical. That night was a soul deposit.

A soul deposit is anything that feeds your soul. You spend so much time and energy on your loved ones, and you're awesome for that. You feed your family's souls each and every day in a million little ways. What do you feed your soul with? Have you forgotten

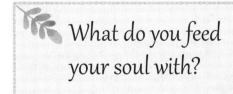

What do you feed
your soul with?

about it? Soul deposits are sort of like the desserts of life, except the more you indulge, the healthier you will be. I sure do wish desserts worked that way as well. I believe the soul yearns for connection, beauty, art, spirituality, nature, awe, play, and truth. The more we feed it those things, the more content we feel.

Happiness Habit

Write today's soul deposit in the lines below. I recommend repeating this exercise in a separate journal each day.

Journal Prompts

1. Think of a time you felt totally at peace. What were you doing?

2. What feeds your soul? How can you get more of that?

3. If you already had all the money you would ever need, what work would you do?

4. What did you love to do as a child? Can you find a way to do that again?

5. Notice the things that seem to fill your children's souls as well, and make note of them.

Chapter Eleven

Social Media and the Myth of the Perfect Mom

I suppose there has almost always been something to perpetuate the myth of the perfect mom. The names Carol Brady, Clair Huxtable, and, of course, June Cleaver come to mind. These women did it all with style and grace. Social media has taken this myth to a whole new level, though. We knew the TV moms weren't the real deal—they were merely acting the part. But now we get to compare ourselves daily to the highlight reels of all the mothers in our newsfeeds, real women we see sometimes on a daily basis at work or as we drop our kids off at school.

Every day that we log on to Facebook, Instagram, or any other social media platform, we are likely to see women with immaculate homes, clean counters, organic vegan dinners, gym memberships, perfectly coifed children, and dogs with matching vests. (Why do dogs even need vests?) Some people go to great lengths to put their "perfection" on display while others genuinely (albeit selectively) share happy moments with friends and families, but don't be fooled. Her kids fight. Her vested dog poops on her hardwoods. Behind the social media photos is a mom living real life, and it's guaranteed to not be picture-perfect.

Looking back through my own posts, I see photos of my family gathered around the table playing a card game, memories from our vacation in Florida, my kids with their arms around each other, even a photo of my dogs in Christmas sweaters! (They did look really cute, so forget the dogs-in-vests joke I just made.) Not pictured are the many tears we've cried struggling through hours of homework my kids didn't understand, the Hamburger Helper we had on paper plates for dinner, the argument my boys had, and the one I had with my husband. I didn't share the cookies I burned, the dog pee on my rug, or the panic attack I had in the grocery store. You only get to see a happy sliver of my life on social media. Nearly everyone is just showing happy slivers, and still we hold the whole of our messy lives up in comparison.

In this chapter, I want to address some of the falsehoods we modern moms may buy into, particularly the ones perpetuated on social media since it's become such a big part of our lives. Because we all tend to share our best moments online, we rarely post the tantrums, the arguments, the bad selfie, or the ugly truths. Yet, when we spend a fair amount of time visiting people's online spaces, we get a skewed perception of their realities. We might actually start to believe that their lives are as perfect as their newsfeeds, which can lead to feelings of inadequacy or guilt.

Let's bust the myth of the perfect mom and realize that we do not have to be perfect to be great mothers!

Messes Are Magic

Lots of moms take messes as a personal insult on their housekeeping abilities. I think we should take them as a compliment on our parenting abilities. What fun would a picture-perfect house be anyway? If our homes stayed pristine at all times, our kids wouldn't get to experience the joys of playing and learning. There would be no finger painting at the table, no juice spills from the toddler who tried to pour it herself, no puddles on the bathroom floor where the bubbles overflowed during rubber-ducky racing, no sticky counters from mixing up ingredients and cooking with Mom or Dad. There'd be no piles of blocks that unleash creativity, no crayon marks where he went off the page, and no toys left in stray places. There'd be few signs that childhood was happening at all. A messy house is a lived-in, loved-in, having-fun-in house. It's not picture-perfect, but it's perfectly wonderful.

I am the first to admit that big messes make me cringe. I like things to be orderly, and when they aren't, I get an uptick in anxiety. However, once I accepted that children come with a certain amount of mess, I was able to look at those messes differently. I started snapping photos of the chaos my boys left behind. It helped to remind myself that messes are temporary but memories last. I know that one day, it'll stay neat and tidy around here and I'll wish for the messes again. Don't worry so much about the messes, Mama. They can be cleaned up, and you can get your kids in a great routine of cleanup time so that it isn't all on you.

I used to say no to activities my kids asked to do that were really messy. "No, you can't dump the Lego bin." "No, you can't crack the eggs." I realized all of my noes were stifling them. I started feeling much happier when I changed my perspective to see messes as magic, and it made my kids happier, too. Now I say yes to messes a lot more often. It's more work, but it's also more fun. I don't want to miss out on making happy memories just so my counters stay clean. However, I make sure that everything is back in order by day's end so I can sleep well!

Moms of older kids, can we talk about their rooms for a second? This is not a crisis. It's not indicative that you're raising a slob. It's definitely not a failure on your part. Yes, let's teach our kids to tidy their rooms, but let's not expect perfection, okay? A lot of joy gets sucked out of our lives because we expect our kids to be perfect—perfectly behaved, perfectly tidy, perfectly well-mannered, perfectly self-controlled, and perfectly happy. We can't even attain perfection at our ages, so maybe we can give the kids a little grace, eh? Sometimes you just have to shut the door and walk away, and remember this: If you think his messy room is tough to look at, just wait until it's empty.

The next time you scroll by a photo of someone's perfectly clean and tidy home, remember that happy memories are often made in messy moments. Embrace your toy-filled floor and glitter-covered table for a while, and look for the magic in the messes.

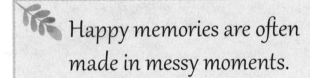

Happy memories are often made in messy moments.

Perfect Siblings

Moms of multiple children often snap pictures of those occasional perfect sibling moments and put them on display for us all to observe. Photos of their little one hugging big brother or gently kissing the newborn. Photos of brothers and sisters playing nicely and videos of happy giggles. It's perfectly understandable to want to capture and share such adorable moments. If my boys are being besties, I want to capture that moment, too! Let's just not deceive ourselves into thinking *her* kids act like that 24–7, and therefore you must have gone terribly wrong somewhere with your kids.

Listen, I think it's very important to teach our kids to respect each other. I'm a big proponent of teaching positive communication and respectful conflict resolution, and of declaring home a safe zone for all who live there. We will have happier, more peaceful families if we teach our children how to treat each other and create clear boundaries on what is unacceptable. However, kids are human! Sometimes they don't like each other very much. They get frustrated with each other. It can be really hard to live in an older sibling's shadow or to feel like you have to compete. So after we've done our best teaching and boundary setting, let's remember again that we can't expect perfect harmony, and let's also remind ourselves that no one who has ever raised more than one child has achieved perfect harmony.

It can be so difficult not to compare our kids to the kids we see online, to not compare their interactions with the interactions in our own homes. It's natural to see those photos and think *I want that,* but it's an illusion. You're looking at a brief moment in time, not a whole story or the complete truth, and that's true for every photo you see. Don't compare yourself or your family to someone else's highlight reel. Your kids won't live a series a picture-perfect moments together, but with patience, growth, and guidance, they will form a strong relationship that's worth so much more than a photograph.

Your Body Is Lovable

We all have that online friend who frequently posts her fitness achievements, promotes her health products, and brags that she gave up sugar and caffeine months ago. Yay for her, really! Let's support one another and be happy for one another, for sure, but let's not allow their accomplishments to dull our own or make us feel shameful of our bodies. I have a wonderful yogi friend whom I admire greatly. She has inspired me to begin my own yoga practice, but I'm still such a newbie at it. So when I see photos of her strong poses or sculpted arms, I have to remind myself that I'm okay where I am in my journey, too. With some dedication, I'll get there, but everyone has to start somewhere.

You are unique and beautiful. Too frequently, we moms feel so ashamed of our bodies that we stay behind the camera. We take all the photos so that we are never *in* the photos. As women, we've always received the message of what "beautiful" is supposed to look like, and it's hard to love our bodies when they don't measure up to that standard. Your body is miraculous and strong. Be grateful for it. Love it. Love yourself, and let your healthy friends inspire you but never shame you.

Trophy Kids

We were a pretty outside-the-box family for a while. My boys were homeschooled for three and a half years. They were not at all into sports, and it seemed like I had the only kids in the county not bringing home ribbons and trophies every season. Everyone else's children seemed so accomplished, and I worried that I was somehow depriving my kids or making them fall behind in life by not forcing them onto some field. So I talked one of them into playing baseball for a season. He hated it. He finished out the season, but he never wanted to play again. I have to admit, though, there was a small part of me that felt really good when he received that participation medal, like it was an accomplishment we could finally display on his shelf. I felt like we'd joined the club, just for a minute.

There is so much pressure to have our kids involved in things. I know that sports and extracurricular activities can be good for kids, but not every child wants a room full of trophies. Some are perfectly content with a room full of comic books or drawings. The question is, can *we* be content with that? Or do we feel the need to have trophy kids so that we can feel accomplished as parents?

The Perfect Husband

Her husband sent her flowers to work "just because." Her husband washed and waxed her vehicle. Her husband took the kids to a movie so that she could relax. Hands up if you've ever logged off feeling a little irritated at your guy because he isn't up to snuff. It's not just ourselves and our kids who get caught in the line of comparison fire. From the looks of it, plenty of other women are enjoying better marriages, more pampering, and wild romance. Except, we're not really seeing what's happening behind the screens, are we?

I was once very shocked to learn that a woman I know, a wife and mom who seemed to have the perfect life, was in an abusive relationship. It just goes to show that we don't know the parts of people's lives that they don't post about. Rather than comparing your partner to everyone else's, look for reasons to be grateful for what you have and ways to strengthen your relationship.

This brings me to my final point for this chapter.

What Are We Missing?

Comparing ourselves with what we perceive to be the "perfect moms" in our newsfeeds doesn't only cause us to feel bad about ourselves and our families. It causes us to miss out on real connections with real people. A "like" or a heart emoji doesn't equal a real conversation. My mom used to get phone calls from friends. During a phone call, you can hear the excitement in someone's voice. Or the quiver. You can gauge a lot by tone of voice. In a social media–driven world, we've lost that to a certain extent. We've traded in meaningful conversation for quick likes and passing comments. We are superficially connected to hundreds but intimately connected to very few, if any.

We become known to many by our posts, but, as we know, that doesn't reflect who we really are or the lives we really live, and I think this is contributing to more loneliness as moms, not less.

The problem with everyone putting their very best on display is that their very worst is left to fester just beneath the surface, unseen. The things we used to air out in private conversation remain hidden. If all we see is each other's perfection, we are very likely to miss each other's pain. Research has shown that social media is making us feel more alone and isolated, and the more time we spend online, the lonelier we feel. Maybe it's time we use our phones for more than texting and tweeting. Call a friend and share what's really going on for each of you.

Strategy: Contentment

*The real reason we struggle with insecurity is because we
compare our behind-the-scenes with everyone else's highlight reel.*
—Steven Furtick

According to a survey of mothers conducted by Edison Research, 93
percent of us are on some form of social media and are spending
about three and a half hours per day online.[4] First, I'm really surprised by that number. I feel like we could be using some of this time
to nurture ourselves, but also this provides ample time for a lot of
negative comparisons to make their way into our minds. Those negative comparisons can make *our* joys feel smaller.

When I have a grateful heart for the good things in my own life,
my contentment keeps me from getting caught in the comparison
trap. When I hear that familiar voice start to rise up and whisper that
someone else has it better, I shut it down by counting my own joys.
When I'm lovingly admiring my own grass, no one else's can possibly
look greener. That's contentment.

Happiness Habit

Take some time today (and each time you hear that unwelcome
whisper) to lovingly admire your own grass. What are you grateful
for today?

Journal Prompts

1. How much time do you spend on social media per day, and is this time well spent?

2. What are the emotional consequences to comparing yourself or your loved ones to others?

3. So you're not perfect. Write five things that make you a great mom.

4. Think about a mom who you've compared yourself to in the past. What does she have that you envy or long for? Is it something you need and, if so, how can you get it?

5. When you were a kid, did you wish for perfect parents? What did you want most from them?

Chapter Twelve

Without a Village:
Tackling Loneliness

I really struggle with friendships.

I have hundreds of online acquaintances, thousands of Instagram followers, and more than a million followers on my Facebook page, but in the real world, I'm just another lonely mom. It's not even that I'm longing for this giant village; I'd be happy with just two or three friends I could count on—friends who would love my kids, come over for tea, and talk about life and motherhood without being judgmental. Since we moved away from my home and my village, I've been afraid to reach out to people here. To be unnervingly honest, I fear rejection. Mix that fear with my highly sensitive, introverted nature, and you have a perfect recipe for loneliness.

I do want to change that, though. I hope to find my little tribe. Truthfully, the isolation has led to my having moderate to severe bouts of depression, which is not surprising: Decades of research has proven that our social connectedness (real relationships, not just online associations) is closely related to our level of happiness and mental well-being. In fact, research has shown that a lack of social connection is a greater detriment to our health than obesity, smoking, and high blood pressure.

I'm not alone in my loneliness. Unfortunately, many moms are suffering with it. I don't have any hard data to share, but a sampling of online polls shows that somewhere between 55 and 85 percent of moms feel lonely, and one only has to open their ears and listen to the conversations around them to discover that this is a real epidemic among modern moms. The pertinent questions are *Why is this happening?* and *What can we do about it?*

Each of the following reasons for loneliness have rung true for me at some point. Perhaps you will relate to a few as well.

You're at a Different Stage Than Other Parents You Know

I had my children later than most of my friends. So their kids were "big kids" when I had infants and toddlers. When their time had finally come that they were freed up enough to actually hang out again, my busy season with littles was just beginning. It was really difficult to coordinate schedules.

Of course, having kids a bit later in life also means I'm an "older mom." It's hard for me to relate to the twentysomethings who have kids the same age as mine. Most moms my age are getting ready to launch their birdies from the nest, so they are also in a very different place than where I am. I'm not saying that I can't form solid friendships with younger moms or moms of young adults. I'd actually love to glean knowledge from those moms of teens and swap stories with the younger ones. It's just that being at different stages of parenthood makes connecting in the first place more challenging, particularly in this new community.

It's Difficult to Find a Friend Who Shares Your Beliefs and Values

I've never really fit into a box neatly. I'm an odd mix, and I am well aware of it. I'd be hard-pressed to find another soul on earth who shares my views. The biggest barrier is that I don't exactly follow the societal norms on parenting, and I've had other moms take offense at that. Some moms have thought I was judging them for their choices just because I chose something different for my family. I get tired of explaining to people that I can parent my way and you can parent yours, and we can still love each other regardless of those choices. It just gets exhausting sometimes trying not to step on people's toes or offend them in some way.

It seems to me that we've gotten to this weird place in our culture where people feel they can't like or associate with someone if they disagree on an issue, any issue! Not only is this absurdity exacerbating our loneliness, but it's causing people to miss out on different perspectives, a wonderful diversity of knowledge and experience, and getting to know some really, really awesome people.

I appreciate the need for like-minded friends. I think it's very helpful to have someone who gets you and your views. The two women I consider my soul sisters both share many of my views. Conversations with them are validating and smooth. Still, though, there is room in our lives and in our hearts for people who believe differently from us, and if there isn't, we've taken a dreadfully wrong turn as a society.

Honestly, I can be your friend no matter what your political affiliation is or belief about how we came to be on this planet. I can love and respect you if you make different parenting choices. Our differences make us unique, and there is so much we can learn from knowing each other. I'm just having a really difficult time finding other people who feel this way, too.

You've Tried but Had No Luck

Maybe, like me, you've tried to reach out, only to be snubbed. Rejection hurts, and it doesn't take many stings before you refuse to go near the hive again, if you know what I mean. It's difficult enough to put yourself out there, to strike up a conversation with a stranger or invite someone over for the first time. When you don't ever hear from them again, it's like a slap in the face. I'm always left wondering what I said wrong or why she felt I wasn't friend material. It just makes me feel bad about myself, and I'm really timid about reaching out now for fear of being rejected again.

I still keep in touch with my best friend from high school. She has that magnetic charm that just seems to draw people to her wherever she lives. She recently moved again and has already created lots of beautiful friendships with local moms. I asked her how she finds a village so quickly everywhere she goes. She replied, "I don't hesitate to walk up to people and ask them for their life story. Most of the time, they like it and we become great friends." That takes confidence and courage that I'm unfortunately still lacking, though we could take a lesson from my charismatic friend. Be bold. Be vulnerable.

Which leads me to my next point: self-confidence. I think this ranks very close to the top of reasons for my own loneliness. I've struggled with my self-confidence since childhood, which has probably caused many missed friendship opportunities.

You Have Low Self-Confidence

If you don't feel like you're bringing anything to the table, you're going to be less likely to reach out to someone. My bashed-up confidence has me constantly doubting myself. Why would they want to be friends with me anyway? I'm not hip. I'm working on valuing myself more, but it's a slow process. That mouthy critic in my brain has been difficult to silence, and I'm having to rewire years of self-doubt and shame messages. Of course, each time I have reached out and been rejected, it's knocked me down a notch. Still, by repeating to myself on a daily basis that I am worth getting to know, it is making a difference. I think people who exude self-confidence, like my high school friend, are the least likely to be rejected, and if they do get rejected, they probably don't take it so personally. I can't expect other people to like me until I like me.

I'm a work in progress.

You'd Have to Give Up Your Few Moments of Alone Time

This is not the case for me now, but I didn't get much alone time at all for the first decade of mothering. I started working from home when my firstborn turned one, and from that point on, I was basically with my children all day, every day, until my oldest was ten. I was a co-sleeping, homeschooling mama for years, and I'm not complaining at all, because those were choices I made (and would happily make again), but it did mean that my alone time was little and precious. We sensitive introverts need our alone time like we need water, and I wasn't about to give that up to go watch a movie with my girlfriends. Priorities!

You've Moved Away from Home

Like so many others, we had to follow work. When my husband's job led us to a new state, I hadn't realized the emotional toll it would take. Being dropped onto new land is scary. When I was home, even if I started talking to a stranger, we had common ground. We could talk about the schools we graduated from, the places we grew up, and area happenings. If I didn't know them, there was a good chance that I knew someone who knew them. Small towns are fun that way. Here in the big city, these types of conversations are challenging. I still have to use my GPS to get to my sons' activities, for crying out loud. I don't know where folks here grew up or went to school.

I miss country roads and familiarity. I miss taking my kids to their grandparents' house to make waffles and my parents being able to drop by and help out when I'm sick. I miss passing by my old high school, visiting familiar playgrounds, and hiking in a forest I know. Most of all, I miss the moms I'd come to know and count on through our years of homeschooling and going to co-op classes. Basically, I miss belonging. That's what it boils down to. We just want to belong.

You Don't Fit In with the Cliques

I always thought the cliques would end after high school, but sadly that isn't the case. Too often, it can feel like moms have their own packs, and it's not always clear if they're welcoming recruits. It's hard to insert yourself into a well-established group of friends. I get it. They've all known each other forever, probably. Their kids have grown up together. It can be hard to welcome the new mom, which isn't all that much different from being the new kid.

I never really was part of the in-crowd. There's no sense in starting at forty, I suppose. Like my kids, I just need to find one or two quirky moms who love *Harry Potter* and orchestra music, and I'll be fine.

Budget

Certainly it would be easier to make mom friends if I had lots of money to throw around. There are plenty of group activities offered in my city, but they're not cheap! I could mingle with the painter moms, the skater moms, or the Zumba moms if only I wanted to cough up the cash required to join. Though I'm not sure that shaking my hips in a very unrhythmic manner is going to make anyone point me out and say, "I want to be friends with that one!"

You're Parenting Alone

Parenting solo is a job like no other. For a couple of years, my husband traveled a lot for work, and I got only a small amount of insight as to what it must be like to parent without a partner. I have such great respect for single moms and moms who have to pull most of the load because her partner must spend so much time away. After you pour so much of yourself into parenting, there is so little time and energy left to build or maintain friendships, and yet it is single moms who perhaps need the village most of all.

Your Kids Keep You Booked

Could it be that there's hardly a day on your calendar that doesn't have something already penciled in? When you have multiple kids into multiple different activities, it can keep your schedule zipped up pretty tight. Finding a blank square to get together with a friend is nearly impossible as it's likely her calendar looks a lot like yours. If you've taken on so much that you don't have time for cultivating these relationships, though, it's probably time to take another look at your schedule.

You Don't Want to Seem Forward or Needy

I don't want to really admit to the moms around here that I'm lonely (although if they read this book, the cat's out of the bag) because I'll feel really pathetic. I don't want a pity date. I also don't want to seem too forward by offering that we get together sometime or awkwardly put them on the spot. Just sending someone a friend request on social media is stressful enough.

Sometimes adult life feels just like middle school life, but with more coffee.

You're an Introvert

I want close friends, but the idea of a moms' night out with several people or doing large group activities doesn't excite me. I much prefer one-on-one conversation or very small, intimate gatherings. Big crowds and lots of hoopla drain me more than they lift my spirits. I'm also not great at small talk. Unfortunately, most people seem to feel uncomfortable with talking about more than the superficial "this weather sure is crazy" stuff.

Where are my people? Where can I find women who want to talk about the deep stuff?

Finding Where We Belong

Mamas, if we want to thrive in motherhood, we have to be brave enough to create our own villages. I have come to believe that

> ## We have to be brave enough to create our own villages.

suffering with loneliness is greater than suffering with the discomfort of putting yourself out there and facing possible rejection.

In a post titled "In the Absence of "the Village," Mothers Struggle Most," Beth Berry speaks so eloquently about this lack of a village on her Web site, Revolution from Home. In it, she says, "We're forced to *create* our tribes during seasons of our life when we have the least time and energy to do so." Yes, that is the crux, isn't it? We need others to show up without our having to jump through hoops to get them there, the way it used to be. She asserts that the absence of the village is distorting many mothers' sense of self because we feel it is our inadequacies, not our circumstances, that are to blame for our struggles.

We were not meant to raise children like this. We were never meant to carry the load on our own, but in this modern day, we have been forced to pick up and carry more than we are capable of. Then we feel inadequate because we struggle to carry it when the problem isn't our own strength but the heaviness of the load. Children used to be brought up in multigenerational communities with aunts, uncles, cousins, and grandparents. There were friends for the kids to roam around with, and mothers had helping hands and listening ears. The children had "bonus moms" to help look after them so that the responsibility of raising a human being wasn't solely on one or two people. There were real, soul-nourishing conversations happening on the front porch. This is how we should be—together.

Sadly, unless you luck into a great deal of money that affords you to buy an entire city block to move your closest family and friends to, the reality that once was is but a dream now. If we want that village, we have to work hard for it by cultivating connections wherever we have been planted.

Strategy: Cultivating Connection

In an ideal world, we'd all stop our mad rush for *more* and rejoin each other once again. We'd put down our cell phones and our overstuffed calendars so that our hands would be free to hold each other's. We'd decide to lay aside our differences and embrace each other as brothers and sisters in humanity. Ideally, you'd see how I'm doing not by visiting my Facebook wall but by sitting within the walls of my home and asking. I'd see your children not on my Instagram feed but outside my window, playing with my children.

Perhaps one day, we will collectively find our way back to each other. Until then, we must individually find our way to the hearts of those around us. We must reach across the miles with real phone calls and actual letters. We have to stop communicating in 280 characters and instead listen to each other's voices again. If we truly want the village back, we each need to do our part in cultivating it. Dr. Brené Brown said, "In the absence of love and belonging, there is always suffering." The way out of loneliness—out of suffering—is love and belonging. To both give it and receive it is the simple yet hard answer.

Fall in Love with You

Dr. Brown talks in her books about belonging to yourself. I believe the first person I need to extend love and belonging to is myself, and that's where I plan to begin. I hope you'll begin here, too, if you have difficulty with self-confidence or self-acceptance. When I love myself, I know my worth. Therefore, it doesn't hinge on whether or not you call me or agree with my views or think I'm cool.

I want this for my children so badly. I want them to love themselves and to know who they are at their core so that they are unshakable. I don't want their self-worth to be dependent upon their peers' opinions, their academic or athletic abilities, the number of social media followers they have (when they are finally allowed to get on social media), or anything at all. I don't ever want their self-worth to be up for debate. So why is mine? What am I teaching my kids with my own actions and beliefs? Once again, my children are helping me rise up.

Practice Vulnerability

Once I love me, I have to be vulnerable enough to love you and to let love in. It's no secret that love can hurt. We've all felt its bite at some point. It's not a mystery that rejection stings. The only way to stand with courage and face the potential heartache is with enough self-love and self-acceptance to know that I'm still likable even if you don't like me. I have to be willing to open myself up again and again in order to find my tribe, because if I'm closed off and hiding the real me, how will my tribe know me when they see me? They won't. If I show up trying to fit in by liking what you like and talking how you talk, I might find a false acceptance, but then I'll need to keep up the facade to keep a friend. I'd rather just be authentic so that I know the connection is real. That takes vulnerability.

Give, Serve, and Volunteer

Not only has giving back been proven to increase your happiness, but it's really a nice way to get to know like-minded people. When you volunteer or serve others, it increases your sense of connection. It makes you feel like you are a part of the community.

Here are some simple ways you and I can get involved in our communities:

1. Shop locally. Visit your locally owned bookstore for purchases and events. Get to know the folks who work there, if you can. This is usually a great hub for community spirit.

2. Cheer on your local sports teams.

3. Donate food to the local food pantry.

4. Visit the shelters and offer your time or used items.

5. Donate used books to local libraries.

6. Organize a block-wide yard sale.

7. Join a running club or other interest group.

Reassess Your Priorities

We often feel busier than we actually are. If we are spending an average of three and half hours per day on social media, dare I say we have enough free time to call a friend or to gather items in a donate box? I tend to put off doing things that make me uncomfortable, even if I really want to do it. Who doesn't? I complain about wanting it but I don't really make it a priority. So, of course, it doesn't happen.

Connection isn't something we can put off without paying a hefty price, though. This one needs to go at the top of the list, even if it feels hard or scary. Cultivating connection will protect your emotional and mental well-being, and that, my friends, is worth the effort.

Happiness Habit

Choose one of these strategies for cultivating connection and make an effort today to do it. What will you do today?

Journal Prompts

1. I listed twelve reasons for loneliness in this chapter. Which ones resonated with you the most? Is there something I didn't mention here that is getting in your way?

2. On a scale of 1 to 10, with 1 being not at all and 10 being tops, how much do you love yourself?

3. Thinking of something you've been interested in getting involved in but haven't made a move yet? What's one small step you could take today?

4. What does your ideal world look like?

5. What kind of village are you looking for? Be specific.

Chapter Thirteen

Introversion and High Sensitivity

The shots rang out again and again; the deafening explosions of the bullets leaving their chambers echoed in my head. I covered my ears like a child, a feeble attempt at blocking out the sounds of horror. There was blood everywhere, coloring the pavement red, and the sight of it made my stomach churn. I felt light-headed and unstable on my legs as I walked away, leaving the crowd, the carnage, and my love behind. I sought refuge in a dingy bathroom stall. Closing my eyes, relishing the quiet, I steadied my breaths and counted backward from sixty. I was brought out of my reverie by the sound of a toilet flushing.

I wasn't caught in a war zone. This was my experience in a crowded theater, watching a violent movie with my husband. I hate violent movies. Loud noises, flashing lights, a crowd—it was a recipe for a disaster from the get-go, but I wanted to go on a date and do "normal" things, like watch a film and eat dinner. I hadn't realized the title we'd chosen would be quite so murderous and brutal.

I'm in that lucky 15 to 20 percent of the population that has the trait of high sensitivity. This means that I feel things deeply, experiencing great pain, great joy, and everything in between. I become easily overwhelmed, either by too much sensory input or having too much to do. I'm very affected by smells, and strong or unpleasant smells are a complete assault on my senses. I seem to absorb the emotions of those around me, even when "those around me" are on a screen. I am easily able to "read" people. It's sort of like having my very own "spidey sense," but not nearly as cool. Although I cannot physically climb walls, my high sensitivity has certainly caused me to climb my fair share of figurative ones.

Do you remember this part in *How the Grinch Stole Christmas?*: "Oh, the noise! Oh, the Noise! Noise! Noise! Noise!" I relate to that whacky green Who. When I am in a loud, chaotic environment like a crowded mall or a fireworks display, I can quickly spiral into grouchiness, too. It's not that I'm confined to my quarters, though. I can enjoy loud concerts and such, but I must retreat immediately after and have a good amount of quiet alone time.

Like other sensitive people, I cry at commercials and beautiful art, and I can be deeply moved by music and poetry. I react very strongly to criticism and can harbor hurt for days afterward. Big decisions stress me out. My wide array of exercise DVDs confirms that I prefer to work out alone, and if you buy me a gym membership, I'll trade it in for a cup of coffee. As it were, I also prefer to work alone, which makes writing in my room a wonderful occupation. But wait, is that because of my introversion or my high sensitivity? They often overlap, and I can't tell which is which.

Yes, along with my high sensitivity, I also happen to be an introvert. In fact, if introversion were on a sliding scale, I'd be toes off the ledge on the "extremely introverted" side. Add my social anxiety to that cocktail and you can imagine how fun I am at parties. That's a joke; of course I don't go to parties. I don't need to; there's a party happening inside my head 24–7. By party, I mean eighty thousand thoughts gathering for tea in the common room, all mingling about. We introverts live inside our heads. In her book *The Secret Lives of Introverts: Inside Our Hidden World,* author Jenn Granneman describes introversion succinctly. She says, "Introverts live in two worlds: We visit the world of people, but solitude and the inner world will always be our home."

Being a highly sensitive introvert has it pluses, too. I'm empathetic and compassionate. I genuinely care for humanity and animals. I might not be a hoot at parties, but we can have a deep conversation for hours about life. I want to help others be happy, and I hope to leave a little light in the places I've been.

The Highly Sensitive Mother

My traits have greatly affected my motherhood, both wonderfully and unpleasantly. Being intuitive, conscientious, and empathetic makes me a better mom. I often know what my kids are feeling before they have even had a chance to verbalize it. I put myself in their shoes often, and this has helped me see things from their perspective and relate to them better. My heart just bursts with love and pride for them. I feel the joys of motherhood intensely. I've been able to find creative ways to teach them and to inspire their own creativity. Because I'm also raising a highly sensitive introverted son, I'm able to understand him in ways no one else can, even if sometimes our high emotions collide.

This brings me to the challenges of being a highly sensitive mother. Motherhood is a roller-coaster ride for the senses. Children are, by their wonderful natures, very loud. They are exuberant, spirited, energetic, and did I mention that they are loud? My ears have been subjected to both quiet coos and high-pitched screams. My nose has experienced a plethora of smells, from light and sweet baby shampoo to dirty diapers and chunky vomit. My eyes have witnessed bloody noses that nearly made me faint but also the sight of a peacefully sleeping baby that I grew inside my own body. It is simply amazing. I've tasted sweat from forehead kisses and the "banana milk" experiment my seven-year-old made in a dusty teapot. I've experienced the gentle caresses of a loving toddler and the painful yank of a fistful of hair.

Many times, I've been overstimulated from the barrage of sensory information to the point of being completely frazzled and utterly touched out. The need to escape to find peace and quiet is very real for sensitive moms, but the means to do so are often very limited, particularly when your children are young. The overstimulation leads to feelings of emotional overwhelm, and this can cause you to get irritable. Because of your sensitive and often perfectionistic nature, you may carry guilt both for feeling the need to escape and for becoming agitated, possibly to the point of yelling or locking yourself away in the bathroom for several minutes. You may wonder why you can't handle things better.

Is a light bulb going off for you as you read this? Perhaps you didn't realize that your sensitivity was an innate trait that you cannot help having. Maybe you've been told your whole life that you are "too sensitive" and you thought that meant you just weren't enough or something was wrong with you. Maybe you didn't realize it was an "actual thing" that others experience as well and that you are completely validated in your feelings.

Psychologist and author of *The Highly Sensitive Person,* Elaine Aron, says that our nervous systems are very sensitive. She asserts that HSPs (highly sensitive persons) process everything around us more than the other 80 percent do. Ask yourself the following questions to determine if you might be highly sensitive, and look into Aron's Web site and books for information and insight into your superpower.

- Do you get rattled when you have a lot to do in a short amount of time?

- Does clutter make you irritable or anxious?

- Do you make a point to avoid violent movies or TV shows?

- Do you notice subtleties in your surroundings that most people miss?

- Did you get told often that you were sensitive as a child?

- Do certain fabrics and textures bother you?

Are you also introverted? Some of the "symptoms" overlap, so it may be difficult to determine which one you are, but they do often go hand in hand.

- Are you more focused on internal thoughts and moods than on external stimuli?

- Do you feel drained after social interaction and need to recharge?

- Are you quiet around unfamiliar people but sociable around people you know well?

- Are you introspective?

- Are you a daydreamer?

- Do you crave at least a bit of solitude each day?

Sanity Savers for Sensitive Moms

There are adjustments you can make as a sensitive and/or introverted mom that will help you feel significantly happier. Self-care is important for all mothers, but it is absolutely essential for highly sensitive moms, and we'll talk more about that in the next chapter. Here are six sanity savers that have helped me to manage my sensitivity.

1. **Identify your triggers.** Pay attention to what overwhelms your senses. When you understand yourself better and become aware of the feelings and sensations in your body as it relates to your environment, you can adjust to minimize or possibly avoid certain triggers altogether.

2. **Create a sanctuary.** I turned my bedroom into a calm and delightful area with ambient lighting and a soft comforter, and I filled it with books. If you can't transform a whole room, take over a small area. Fill it with things that are pleasing to your senses, such as a soft pillow or a lightly fragranced candle. Listen to something calming or inspiring.

3. **Know what reenergizes and refocuses you.** Just as important as identifying your triggers is identifying your strengtheners. Listening to a chapter of an audiobook, taking a walk outside, or playing music while I take a hot shower all help me get re-centered. It's essential that you build in a little time each day to do what fills you up.

4. **Organize your spaces and keep them clutter-free.** Believe me, I know this is a challenge when you have kids. Their bedrooms and playroom are a different story, but the main living areas I dwell in—the living room, kitchen, and my bedroom—are kept relatively tidy. It seems that my head space is directly related to my living space. If one is cluttered, they both are. Is it just me? All I know is that I feel much more at peace when everything is in its place.

5. **Learn to honor your sensitive self and live a slower, more intentional life.** It's okay to say no to that invitation if you know it's going to drain you. You don't have to have your kids signed up for every sport and extracurricular that comes around. You're not obligated to help run everything

you're involved in. When we are stretched too thin, it takes a toll on our already sensitive nervous systems, and when there are no blank spaces in the calendar, there is no room for cozying around and recharging.

6. **Build in calming connection time with your kids.** This has been a vital step for me because I'm raising two boys, one of whom is very exuberant (read: loud and energetic). There is a time for Nerf wars and having light saber battles, but every night I bring them into my sanctuary for thirty to sixty minutes of reading aloud and chatting, even though they are big boys now. The only light is my book light. It's a relaxing way to end the day. This has become a favorite ritual for all of us.

Strategy: Honor Who You Are

I personally believe highly sensitive people are an asset to society. We make the very world that often overwhelms us softer, kinder, and brighter. Our strengths are needed to remind people to slow down, quiet down, feel the emotions they've pushed down, trust their instincts, and be aware of the world around them.

There is nothing wrong with you, Mama. Honor who you are, come to love the person you see in the mirror, appreciate your traits, and see your sensitivity as a superpower. You are more attuned than 80 percent of the world, and that makes you pretty special. Welcome to the club. We will not be having meetings.

Learn to accept all the parts of you so that you can accept all the parts of your children. Maybe you're raising a sensitive child like I am. If we can give a sensitive child one gift that will help in every aspect of growing up, it's self-love. Yet you know we cannot give that which we do not possess.

The first step in honoring yourself is forgiving yourself what you did not know and could not help. If you'd have known that clutter and noise would have a negative effect on your senses, you could have prepared, but we all are learning as we go in motherhood. Forgive yourself for your irritability. It doesn't make you bad, and now you can use the tools I listed to help you be calmer. Forgive yourself for needing a little solitude. There is nothing wrong with that, and your children will be just fine in another trusted adult's care for thirty minutes while you reset your nervous system.

Understand that these traits are part of you but they do not define you and they do not limit you. You can still be rowdy with your kids, take a trip to the ever-crowded theme parks, and enjoy a road trip with your family. You just have a take a little extra tender care of yourself along the way. Listen to your body and mind. Honor your needs. Get out there and enjoy your life. Remember, you are the mother your child needs. You are the mother your child loves.

Happiness Habit

Exercise regularly. I know everyone says it, but it really is helpful. The value of exercise cannot be overemphasized for sensitive moms. Exercise reduces stress, refreshes both the mind and body, and releases endorphins that make you feel happier. Exercise also increases your oxygen intake, energizing you.

While competitive sports and crowded gyms may not be for you, there are plenty of HSP-friendly options for improving fitness and recharging yourself. Good options include Pilates, hiking, swimming, biking, and gardening.

Journal Prompts

1. Where in your home can you create a little sanctuary?

2. Set your creativity free. What can you create today?

3. What does the word *sensitivity* mean to you? Does it have positive or negative associations in your mind?

4. List the ways you think your sensitive nature is a gift to others.

5. How can you prioritize exercise in your day-to-day life?

Chapter Fourteen

Practical Self-Care

Before my children were born, I had a pretty predictable daily flow. Eating, sleeping, showering—these are done on my terms and in my own time. I enjoyed hobbies, date nights with my husband, and outings with friends at my leisure. My husband and I could decide on a last-minute weekend getaway with little more than a duffel bag to pack. On the weekends, we stayed up really late and slept in the next morning. Do you even remember the last time you woke up to your own internal clock?

For several years, we worked opposite shifts. This meant that when I got home from work, I had the entire evening to myself almost every day. I enjoyed an hour-long exercise routine each day. I did regular hair treatments, facial masks, and foot soaks. I went shopping to buy clothes for myself, if you can imagine that. Self-care certainly wasn't an issue, so it was a big shock to go from having all evening to myself to having almost no time to myself.

When my son was born, he was the greatest gift I'd ever been given, but he also turned our lives upside down. Suddenly, I ate, slept, and showered on his terms. His needs, of course, came before mine, and because infants need a lot, I rarely had time to meet my own. My hobbies became a thing of the past. Outings with friends were no longer a priority. Date nights with hubby became few and far between. I shopped for baby, sang for baby, stayed up for baby, woke up for baby—my whole world revolved around my little bundle of joy.

For a long time, I thought that putting my needs at the top of the list was a selfish thing to do. *It's not about me anymore*, I told myself. I thought I was being a good mommy by sacrificing my needs, but really, my actions had more to do with guilt than with a true lack of time. I could have put him down more and he would have surely been just fine. I could have left him with grandparents or sitters to go out with my husband. I could have left him with my husband to go see a friend. I chose not to do those things because, in my mind, a good mom was *all* about her kids. This isn't only a false idea but a dangerous one, as it causes mamas to neglect themselves to the point of totally empty cups.

At the time, I do remember thinking that the self-care ideas that I came across were pretty unrealistic, though. They required me to "sleep when the baby slept," but I just physically couldn't, no matter how tired I was. They told me to get up hours before my children to have free time alone in the mornings, but I co-slept with my kids so when I got up, it woke them up. They told me to put my kids to bed and enjoy an evening with my husband, but my kids needed me to lie with them for years. By the time they fell asleep, I was often asleep myself. I was so exhausted by day's end, I hardly had the energy or desire to knit or read a novel.

Sure, I could have changed my children's sleep habits. I could have made different decisions, but being available at night was important to me, and anything else wouldn't have been true to my values as a mother. The long nights were tiring, but they also built a beautiful foundation with my kids. Those nights that I lay with them before sleep were filled with imaginary trips to faraway galaxies; stories about dragons, knights, and sacred gems; back rubs; and sweet cuddles. I wouldn't trade them for all the candlelit bubble baths in the world.

I learned an important lesson about self-care during those early years as a mom. The first is that it is absolutely necessary and not selfish to take care of my own needs. The second is that I could redefine what self-care meant *for me*. I had to examine the ideas I had in my mind about what self-care was supposed to look like because, honestly, part of what left me feeling deprived was my unrealistic expectation that self-care had to be stolen hours from my previous life.

Date night didn't have to be a fancy dinner and a two-hour movie at the theater. It could be twenty minutes of sitting across from each other at our little dining room table with a lit candle and a couple of Hot Pockets. What truly mattered was that we were connecting. Catching up with friends didn't have to mean a book club meeting at the café or a scrapbooking party at someone's house. It could look like a ten-minute FaceTime chat to catch up with each other. What truly mattered was that we were connecting. I could be just as rejuvenated by laughing during our nightly space adventures as I was by pampering myself for an hour with a deep-conditioning treatment and polishing my nails. It was really a matter of perspective and yes, of course, gratitude.

Once I let go of my unrealistic ideas about self-care, it became easy to find practical acts that nourished my mind, body, and spirit. That's really what self-care is, after all. It doesn't have to look a certain way or last a certain length of time. I can sit a cup on the counter and walk by every couple of hours to pour a little water in. By the end of the day, the cup will be full. The same principle applies to self-care. I can pour in a little at a time throughout the day and still end up full of joy.

There's Not Enough Time!

I completely understand the feeling that there is simply no time for self-care. I used to feel that way, too. However, I think if you crunch some numbers, you might be surprised to find a little extra in there to work with. We get 168 hours per week. Take a few minutes to add up the amount of hours you work per week, sleep per week, and spend at commitments like church or sports per week. Then monitor how much per day you actually spend on social media or perusing the Internet. It's such a time suck that we don't often realize how long we scroll and read on there. When I paid close attention to my time, I discovered that, when I added the time I spent on the Internet with the time I played useless games on my phone (neither of which nurtured my mind, body, or spirit), I was wasting at least an hour each day that I could have been using to care for myself.

Dear reader, you need to understand that you are an important human being who means the world to someone. You matter not only because you are a mom, but because you are *you*. Your physical, mental, and spiritual well-being matters. You know that you cannot pour from an empty cup, so take time each day to fill up so that you not only give the best to your family but so that you can live your one

> You cannot pour from an empty cup.

life well. Taking care of yourself wasn't a selfish thing to do before you had children, and it's not selfish now. You are still a person with needs! Self-care isn't about saying "I'm more important than you." It's about saying, "I'm important, too." I'm not suggesting you put your needs above your child's at all, just that you put your needs back at the top of your priority list.

What Nurtures You?

Do you have realistic ideas about self-care? What does self-care mean to you? It's helpful to look at your expectations and break them down. Are they reasonable or achievable? I used to look at self-care as "time away" or "time to myself," and those are important to have sometimes, but there are plenty of ways to add a little bit to my cup several times throughout the day without having to leave my house or be alone. When you open your eyes to all the small possibilities, nurturing yourself isn't just a lengthy ritual you can only hope for. Rather, you can nourish yourself in little ways all throughout the day right in the midst of your busy life. All you need is a shift in perspective and a declaration to take care of you.

Choose acts that truly nourish *you*. What one mom considers self-care may actually add stress to another mom. Take into account your personality. It may even be helpful to take some personality tests as these can offer unique insight into what makes you tick. Getting to know yourself better may help you understand why a certain self-care routine would help you more than another. You may discover that your personality type explains why you put others' needs ahead of your own. Personality tests can also help you identify your strengths, and you can use that information as you form your personalized self-care routine.

The Myers-Briggs Type Indicator is one of most popular and, in my opinion, helpful personality tests there is. Others you may find useful are the Enneagram, the Color Code Personality Assessment, and the Winslow Personality Profile. According to the Myers-Briggs Type Indicator, I am an INFJ. This means I am introverted, intuitive, feeling, and judging. Further study into this personality type reveals that, for example, I place great importance on having things orderly and systematic. Knowing this, I can make clutter reduction part of my self-care routine because I know that I feel better internally when my external world is neat and tidy. I can also purchase a great planner to help me keep my commitments and goals in order, which is also a form of self-care for my personality type. Knowing who you are will help you take better care of yourself.

Here are some practical ways you can nurture yourself each day.

1. **Exercise.** I know you were expecting this one, but stay with me. You may not be able to make it to the gym for an hour or go for a run. I used to think that if I couldn't work out like I used to pre-kid, then I couldn't really work out. I was so used to doing my hour-long DVDs during my alone time in the evenings before I had children that other options didn't really occur to me. I just saw that I couldn't do what

I used to do as it required room, equipment, and a block of time that was difficult to get with a baby to care for. Of course, another *big* problem was energy. Getting choppy sleep every night didn't exactly leave me feeling like doing jumping jacks. However, time and time again, I've found that if I can just make myself start, the energy will come.

What really helped me was to realize that my exercise didn't have to look a certain way. As long as I moving my body, that was good enough, so might I recommend to you that you aim for "good enough" exercise? Some options to try are stretching on the floor next to your baby, throwing in twenty jumping jacks and ten lunges on each side before you fold those onesies in the hamper, or having a dance party with your toddler. Even taking five to ten minutes to stretch, jog in place, or do burpees is getting your blood pumping. If you do these short exercises several times throughout the day, it'll make a difference in how you feel. For added benefit, research has found that working out for as little as twenty minutes can trigger the release of endorphins, those happy hormones that lower stress and promote positive feelings.

2. **Play.** Sometimes we tend to look at playing with our kids as a chore, but it is possible to train your mind to see play as a positive experience you share with your kid, not just something you have to check off the list. To combat the boredom, find ways to play with your child that you actually think are fun! Let your inner child out to play! Jump in puddles. Paint together. Sled down hills and make up silly songs. Try to

remember what you loved to play as a child and do that again.

Too many adults have forgotten how to play. We take everything so seriously, with all our great responsibilities and busy agendas, but play isn't just for children. In fact, adults greatly benefit from playing. Darcia Narvaez, PhD, says, "Our right hemisphere can grow throughout life and play is one of the best ways to grow it! Systems governed by the right hemisphere include self-regulation of various kinds and intersubjective responsiveness (emotional presence with others). These are fundamental to happiness and compassionate morality."[5]

3. **Drink lots of water.** How is your water intake? We all know that drinking enough water is good for physical health, but what about our mental health? Studies have shown that even mild dehydration is enough to cause moodiness, headaches, trouble concentrating, and fatigue. By the time you are thirsty, your body is already dehydrated. While specific guidelines vary, the Institute of Medicine recommends that women consume ninety-one ounces of water each day. This is one of the most basic self-care tips, but it's advice that many of us do not heed. The key takeaway here is that if you want to maintain optimal moods, you should maintain your hydration.

4. **Practice tai chi.** Yoga is often recommended for reducing stress and increasing happiness, but tai chi is a wonderful alternative. Often described as "meditation in motion," it is

a fluid, gentle form of exercise designed to relax the body and refresh the mind. The benefits of tai chi include stress reduction, mental clarity, calmness, increased energy and flexibility, improved muscle strength, and increased feelings of mental well-being.

5. **Dance.** Swedish researchers studied more than one hundred teenage girls who were struggling with issues like anxiety and depression. Half the girls attended weekly dance classes, while the other half did not. The study showed that the girls who danced showed improvement in their mental health and reported a boost in their mood, and these positive effects lasted up to eight months after the dance classes ended. Another study on a small group of seniors reported similar findings, showing that twelve weeks of Zumba led to improved mood and cognitive skills. Dance is good for our mental health, whether we are fifteen or seventy-five! Adding dance to your self-care routine is a promising way to increase your feelings of happiness and well-being.

6. **Keep a book of joy.** The benefits of gratitude journals are well-documented and proven to make you feel happier. A book of joy is your own personalized happiness book. It's anything you want it be! Write what you are grateful for each day as a start, but then keep going. Fill it with doodles of hearts and snapshots of your kids. Write wonderful quotes and profound thoughts. Record funny moments, proud moments, and moments that take your breath away.

Your very own book of joy is a tangible, beautiful, hold-in-your-hands collection of the goodness in your life.

7. **Reduce mental clutter.** As previously discussed, there are too many voices coming from all directions. Clearing your mind allows you to be a more focused, intentional parent. We live in a world in which we are constantly bombarded with opinions and information. Learning to distinguish all of the outside voices from our own is essential to self-care. I recommend setting aside whole days where you do not go online. The break from the constant stream of information is really refreshing and sets a much-needed example to our children about tech responsibility and the importance of caring for one's own mental health. Meditation and prayer are terrific ways to reduce mental clutter as well, and even just short daily practices can have a positive impact on your mental clarity.

The Internet isn't the only source of loud, opinionated voices. You may need to take a break from draining friends or family members as well. If someone's constant and un-wanted advice frequently makes you feel confused or upset, you may need to distance yourself for a while. In addition, any television shows you may be watching or other media you're consuming that is adding to your mental clutter can be put aside while you tune back in to your own voice.

8. **Listen to something inspiring.** I love to feed my mind and soul with uplifting and inspirational podcast episodes, TED talks, orchestra music, and audiobooks. I often have

one ear plugged and one free so that I can hear my children while they're scootering at the park or playing downstairs. Research has found that listening to your favorite music releases dopamine, the same hormone released in response to sex, eating, and certain illegal drugs. Music has also been found to reduce anxiety and literally ease pain. Listening to podcasts, audiobooks, and the like that make you smile and feel more positive is making an intentional choice as to what type of information you are allowing in. In an information-overloaded society, being intentional about the information we consume is critically important.

9. **Write.** Pouring your mind out onto paper is incredibly therapeutic. Expressive writing has been shown to have numerous benefits for the mind and body, even demonstrating the ability to heal wounds faster. James W. Pennebaker, author, along with Joshua M. Smyth, of the book *Opening Up by Writing It Down: How Expressive Writing Improves Health and Eases Emotional Pain,* says, "Writing about an emotionally charged subject or an unresolved trauma helps you put the event into perspective and give some structure or organization to those anxious feelings, which ultimately helps you get through it." Try writing about a tough situation or experience and see if it helps you feel better. On a lighter note, perhaps you would enjoy writing poetry or song lyrics?

10. **Enjoy the little moments intentionally.** Our lives are made up of little moments, yet so many of them go unnoticed in

the hustle of daily diaper changes, work, baths, homework, meals, chores, and so on. If we aren't mindful, we'll miss the beauty in our ordinary days. A lot of people so look forward to the big moments in life (the vacations, the birthdays, the graduations) that they fail to see the joy in the little moments. Every single day presents us with gifts to unwrap and memories worth holding on to. Notice them. Hold in your heart a deep appreciation for these moments as you notice them, and nothing will change you so profoundly. I don't need a day at the spa nearly as much as I need to appreciate the joyful moments that each day with my children brings.

11. **Get creative.** Take up your paintbrushes, pencils, knitting needles, and gardening gloves. Create with your hands. Care for your spirit by unleashing your creativity. Making art has been shown to lower cortisol levels, reducing the stress hormone in the body. Gardening boosts mood. Creating crafts enhances self-esteem. You have an incredible ability to create unique, gorgeous works of art that no one else can create.

12. **Make your spaces beautiful.** I love clean, uncluttered spaces. I love fresh-cut flowers on my dining table. I love ambient lighting. Moms, we live among a splattering of toys, sippy cups, and dirty laundry. As I type this, my table is covered in Lego sets. As the mom of two boys, I understand mess. There is a place for messes—a time to see the magic in the block creations and sticky countertops.

However, I am aware of how my living spaces affect my mental health, and I make it a priority to have some spaces in my home that remain uncluttered, serene, and organized. I need a place where I can escape the toys and the noise, where my introverted, sensitive self can find rest. Decluttering has been shown to improve mental well-being, but you don't have to do it all at once. Start small. Tackle one drawer or corner a day until you live in a space that makes you feel happier.

13. **Learn to say no.** One of the most beneficial acts of self-care is to learn to say no to things you do not want in your life so that you can make more room to say yes to the things that matter most. Moms are nurturers and caretakers. We often try to accommodate everyone because we place such a high value on relationships. How many times have you said yes when you wanted to say no? How many times have you overextended yourself for someone else's benefit? Your time is valuable. No one else will create boundaries to protect your time and energy for you. It's up to you to create and honor healthy boundaries for yourself.

14. **Laugh.** When is the last time you laughed until your sides hurt? How often do your children hear you belly laugh? I was thinking about this question recently, and my answer was "not nearly enough." I want my kids to remember the sound of my laughter just as surely as I will remember theirs. You've already heard about all the amazing benefits

of laughter, but are you seeking it out? Are you looking for reasons to laugh? My boys love to watch those "try not to laugh" videos on YouTube. They have the right idea. They're chasing laughter. I invite you to join me in chasing laughter today.

15. **Pick up a hobby.** If you feel that you have no time to pick up a hobby right now, then you probably need a hobby most of all! Everyone needs a little slice of time devoted entirely to something they enjoy. You do have an identity beyond "mom." Your hobby doesn't need to be expensive or time-consuming. One of the best things I've done for myself in recent years was to buy a new bike and start riding again. I felt like a kid at Christmas!

Strategy: Mini Indulgences

I used to let my inability to achieve big self-care acts (full-body massages, relaxing vacations, a night out with my husband) keep me from indulging in small acts of self-care until I realized there were many different ways to fill my cup, and I could fill it a little at a time all throughout my days. What a revelation! I've just listed fifteen simple acts of self-care that don't require much time or money at all. What else can you add to the list? I encourage you today to brainstorm a list of fifty mini acts of self-care. I believe you'll be pleasantly surprised that nurturing your mind, body, and spirit is easier than you might think.

Happiness Habit

Name *your thing*. Think of one small act that nourishes your mind, body, or soul that you can do every day. Embrace that one thing as yours and make it as much of a priority as brushing your teeth. Name it here:

_____

_____

_____

Journal Prompts

1. What is one activity that you are spending time on each week that *does not* feel nurturing to you? Can you let this activity go or at least decrease it? What would make it less taxing?

2. List ten things that make you smile.

3. What activities feed your soul the most? How can you incorporate these into your life more?

4. Does taking care of your needs ever make you feel guilty? Why?

5. Write three reasons explaining why *you* are worth nurturing.

Chapter Fifteen

Beauty and the Beast: Panic Attacks, Anxiety, and Living in Fear

I awoke with a start. It felt as though a huge, strong, invisible hand was gripping my throat. It was almost impossible to breathe. My chest was heavy, my heart pounding and skipping frantically inside. I was dying. I just knew it. I felt death trying to pull me under as I desperately tried to remain conscious. With widened eyes, I looked at my sweet toddler boy beside me and the thought crossed my mind that I'd never see him grow up. With that, tears sprang into my eyes and exploded down my cheeks as I tried to stand and go to the bathroom. I thought if I could splash my face, it would help me hold on, but the room was wobbly. I was completely disoriented. I yelled for my husband, waking my little boy, who had been sleeping peacefully beside me.

He came sprinting in. "What's wrong?" I was four months pregnant with our second son. "I think I'm dying," I choked out. "Maybe a heart attack or something." He spent the next forty minutes calming me down, coaching me through deep breaths, and holding me close as I begged God to let me live to see my boys grow. My son was clutching me, tears streaming down his face now, too. I scared him so badly that night. It was the most terrifying experience of my life— up to that point. It was my first panic attack.

I've had hundreds more in the nine years since. Several sent to me the emergency room. I remember one ER doctor actually laughed at me when I told him I was dying. I suppose he's never had a panic attack. Imagine coming face-to-face with the thing you most fear, day after day after day. That's what my panic attacks were like. I was terrified of death, and yet I felt it knock on my door nearly every single day. This went on for years despite my many efforts of trying to manage them.

To those who don't understand the terror of a panic attack, I explain it like this. Imagine being afraid of spiders and having someone throw a tarantula on your face often and at random. You never know when the person will throw it on you. The person sneaks up and does it, but you know it's coming. So you start to live in terror—waiting. There is no escape.

It felt like my own little circle of hell.

For the rest of that pregnancy, I was afraid to be alone with my toddler. I feared I'd pass out and he'd be left alone, or that I'd actually die the next time one came on. Horrifying scenarios played out in my mind on a loop. Sometimes I had four or five panic attacks in a day. Soon, every trip to the store brought on a panic attack. I imagined terrible car crashes and dramatic deaths in the produce aisle. I could hardly leave my house. It wasn't always that bad, though. There were times when I thought I may actually be able to return to normal, but that hope was soon annihilated. It seemed that living with panic disorder was my new normal, and I had no idea how to be the mommy my boys needed and deserved while I was constantly fighting this demon. There was so much *beauty* in my life, but this *beast* called anxiety and panic kept me from fully enjoying it.

It has been nearly a decade since my first attack. My symptoms have waxed and waned over the years, mild and manageable at times and completely debilitating at others. I've tried many methods to improve my mental health, and I'm grateful to say that I'm living happily and free from constant fear and panic now. While I may never fully slay this beast and be rid of it forever, I have learned how to manage it and enjoy my life again. I'm finally seeing beauty more than the beast.

Mama, have you struggled with mental health issues, too? I wish we could sit in a coffee shop and talk about this. I want to listen as you pour out all your worries and fears, all your guilt and shame, and I want to tell you that I understand. No judgment. I suppose curling up with this book is the closest we'll probably get, so listen. I want you to know that your mental struggle does not make you a bad parent, and there is hope for healing. You may never be "normal" again, but you can feel better than you do today. You can rise up with new hope and new strength. You can learn to be calmer and happier.

I know firsthand how the constant anxiety can cause you to be irritable with your kids. I know from experience the bone-tired mental exhaustion you feel from constantly fighting, but you keep on fighting anyway for your children and your family. You are a warrior, just like me. We battle demons no one else can see. We face them down every single day with shaky legs and the fierceness of a mother bear protecting her cubs. It scares us to death, but we look them in the eyes and say "Not today! I'm not going down today." It takes an amazing amount of courage, but do we give ourselves credit for that? Not usually. I didn't for a very long time. I only chastised myself for not being strong enough to win the battle for good. Guilt was a constant. The shame was the worst. Overcoming these things in order to live happier takes a warrior's courage, and you have that. You are so much stronger than you give yourself credit for.

Strategy: Take Baby Steps

The first thing I want to encourage you to do is talk to a medical professional. The second thing is to take one small step each day. If you are in the grips of depression or anxiety, one little step is all it takes to start healing. You don't have to conquer this today! You just need to find a tiny bit of courage to move. Maybe that looks like putting on full makeup or sitting outside on the porch for a few minutes. Maybe it looks like driving to the parking lot but not going inside the store. Perhaps it's just going to be picking up the phone to call the doctor's office.

The next thing I need you to know is that relationships can be repaired and people can heal. If you are locked in guilt or shame because your mental struggle has caused you to snap at your kids, say

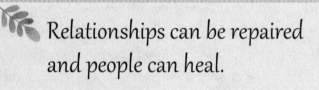

Relationships can be repaired and people can heal.

hurtful things to your loved ones, or just not be present and engaged in their lives and yours like you wanted to be, please give yourself compassion and forgiveness. So many moms remain stuck in the shame loop because they wanted "better" for their family, and believe me, sweet Mama, I get that. I really do.

The thing is, they're waiting for you with open arms. They're waiting for you to come back to them, and they are ready to love you and forgive you. If they're willing to give that to you, can you be willing to give it to yourself? You can't undo the past, but you can move forward and build connections. You can apologize and love them so much that their hearts heal and their souls flourish. You can make enough good memories that the bad ones fade to the back of their minds.

That baby of yours just wants to see his mother's smiling face. You deserve to be happy in your one precious life.

Happiness Habit

Record your one small baby step each day over the next week.

Day one:

_____

_____

_____

Day two:

_____

_____

_____

Day three:

_____

_____

_____

Day four:

_____

_____

_____

Day five:

_____

_____

_____

Day six:

_____

_____

_____

Day seven:

_____

_____

_____

Journal Prompts

1. What are two things you can do now to improve your mental health?

2. What do you wish most people knew or understood about you?

3. Write the words you need to hear.

4. How do you see yourself this time next year? In five years?

5. What is your biggest motivation for improving your mental health?

Living on Alert—Choosing Joy over Fear and Worry

While you may not be living with severe anxiety, panic disorder, depression, or a true mental health concern, fear and worry are happiness stealers that all mothers experience on some level. Pre-kid, I had a carefree spirit. Post-kid, I see the potential danger in everything.

Let me illustrate my point with a story. Every summer, the Internet becomes inundated with articles about dry drowning. I'm sure you've seen them. These articles terrify me and make me extremely paranoid. Fresh off a reading of one of these little gems, my kid started choking while drinking a glass of water. He coughed and sputtered, and I thought this was a medical emergency. After all, I had no idea how much water could have gotten into his lungs, and I'd just read how it only took a tiny bit to cause death. I wasn't going to take any chances. I took my child to the ER. The look on the doctor's face was priceless when I told him I was afraid my son was drowning because he had choked on a drink of water, and I'm sure they had a good laugh about me that night. The threat may have been false, but my fear was very real.

I'm always on hyperalert around water now. Last year, my children went to a school pool party. I stood by the edge of pool trying to watch both my kids at the same time. Perhaps you know how hard it is to keep an eye on two different boys in a large group of kids when they're both going separate ways. Good grief! All the other moms and dads were sitting around tables chatting with one another other while I stood there frantically searching the pool as though it were shark-infested. I saw the strange looks from the other parents, but whatever! *How can they just sit there when their children are clearly in imminent danger?* Someone finally came up to me and asked, "Are you okay?" "Not really, no," I replied. "My kids aren't great swimmers and water makes me nervous." She replied, "Um, but they can stand up in it."

Yeah, so? One gulp of water down the wrong pipe is all it took!

This was, in my opinion and in my heightened state of vigilance, a highly dangerous situation.

From the days of logging all their poops to dropping them off at middle school (current situation), fear and worry have been my side-kicks. Keeping tiny humans alive and safe isn't easy when they want to dart through crowded places, climb everything imaginable, "fly" off the backs of couches, pet strange dogs, and do daring, wild things like drink a glass of water!

Then there are times when things really do get serious.

My son was four years old when it happened. It was an ordinary day when he developed an unordinary limp. It started small and barely noticeable, but it progressed rapidly. Within a couple of hours, he was limping heavily and complaining of pain. He hadn't injured it that I knew of, so I decided to head to our pediatrician's office.

It was a twenty-minute drive to the hospital. By the time we got there, my son could no longer walk. That's how quickly his condition was worsening. I had no idea what was happening. I carried him into the doctor's office and frantically said he needed to be seen right away. On the exam table, it was noted that he had redness and swelling in all his joints, and he cried out in pain when they were touched. His pediatrician determined he had serum sickness due to an antibiotic he was on for strep throat. He recommended he be admitted imme-diately.

Registration for admittance took another thirty minutes or so. I held him on my lap as we waited. He was scared and in pain, and my heart ached for my sweet boy. Once in the room, he was instantly surrounded by a team of nurses who got to work. As they tried more than ten times to get an IV in him and failed, I held his hands and rubbed his head, whispering in his ear that I was so sorry and that I was there for him. Since they couldn't get the IV in, they had to go with oral medication, which they administered, and we waited.

By the next day, he could walk again. In a few days, he was back to his normal, happy, energetic self, but it took me longer to recover emotionally and mentally. For months, I watched him vigilantly. To this day, every swollen lymph node or headache rings an alarm in my head that I have to talk down.

Worry and fear come with the territory in parenthood, but there are things we can do to keep them in perspective. Even general worry has the potential to snatch you right out of a perfectly peaceful now and hurl you into a storm of what-ifs, and once the habit is formed, not worrying feels a bit disconcerting—almost like you're forgetting something important.

Here's the silver lining in the serum sickness story. When my son talks about that experience today, it isn't the fear, the pain, the needles, or the medicine that he remembers. Instead, he remembers that day as "the day Mommy carried me." There is such a beautiful lesson in this story. We all need to be carried sometimes. It's when we toss the shame aside and allow ourselves to be carried that love seeps in and does its healing work. The pain we experience cannot extinguish the love we are gifted as long as we let that love in. During dark times, it is tempting to shut others out. Don't. Let them carry you through so that one day, when you recall the experience, you don't remember the hurt so much as you remember the love.

Strategy: Logical Thinking

Thankfully, there are two simple ways to keep worry from becoming a chronic problem. Noam Shpancer, PhD, recommends asking two main questions.[6] 1) How likely is it, really? When you consider the true odds of your worry coming to pass, you're likely to realize that it isn't worth losing sleep over. 2) How bad is it, really? Our worrying minds have a tendency to catastrophize, so this question brings the brain back into logic.

Dr. Shpancer also emphasizes that you aren't looking to counter negative thoughts with positive thoughts but rather to counter inaccurate thoughts with accurate thoughts. That's an important distinction because the goal isn't to paint everything rosy but to think logically. That way, if there is, indeed, a threat, you can be prepared.

Happiness Habit

Use Dr. Shpancer's strategy for each worry or fear that comes up over the course of reading this book. I'll give you space below to write them out.

What's your worry? How likely is it, really? How bad is it really?

Journal Prompts

1. Write a note that begins with "Dear Fear . . ."

2. Write about one of today's victories or accomplishments.

3. Name something you worried about in the past that never happened.

4. Name someone who has carried you through a difficult time. Write about it.

5. What's the scariest thing that has happened to you? What did you learn from it?

Chapter Sixteen

Laugh Out Loud

My four-year-old son had built an alligator with his Duplo blocks. I could only vaguely make out the shape of an alligator, but I was impressed with his creativity and use of colorful blocks. He was proudly showing it to me, describing in detail how it could jump high up into the sky and come down the chimney (much like Santa). He excitedly told me how it'd crash right into the logs, and as he was talking, his little brother came by and knocked the alligator over. A few blocks came off, but my four-year-old just went on about his business, unfazed. He had grown rather used to such things in the two years he'd been a big brother, I suppose. A few minutes later I asked him what he wanted for Christmas as it was only a few weeks away. He didn't miss a beat when he said sincerely, "An alligator that's not knocked over." Bless him. It was all he asked for.

If you want to be a happier mom, here's an important tip: Don't take yourself too seriously. Laugh at yourself. Laugh with your children. Did you know that laughter truly is strong medicine? It's not just a meaningless saying, it's really true! Laughter boosts your mood, diminishes stress and pain, and strengthens your immune system. Plus, when you laugh together with your children, it's a bonding experience that helps them to release any negative feelings they may be harboring.

Look for opportunities to laugh every single day, and because you have children, you shouldn't have to look very far. Kids say and do the funniest things! I asked parents on my Facebook page to share their hilarious and cute stories, and I'm combining their stories to make this laugh-out-loud chapter for you to reference when you need a little boost in health and happiness. (Note: The names have been changed, but the stories were shared by real moms.)

Stick your bookmark in this page, and come back whenever you need a good laugh.

Every mom has a funny story to share. Here is a fair warning to new moms: Your child will eventually embarrass you in public. As you read these next few stories, just thank your lucky stars they didn't happen to you. Yet!

Dawn shares the perils of taking her toddler son into a public restroom. She says, "I was at the grocery store with my toddler son. I needed to use the restroom, so I had to take him in with me. I told him to hold my purse and face the wall so I could have a bit of privacy. A minute later, he turned around and loudly said, 'Mom! Why do you pee out of your butt?' The lady in the next stall started laughing. I was too embarrassed to show my face, so I waited until the entire bathroom was empty before I made my quick exit."

And speaking of bathroom funnies, Abby's little girl was not shy about getting her needs met. No, sir. She shares, "When my daughter was three, she insisted on using a public bathroom stall by herself. I was standing right outside it, and when she got done, she yelled for the whole restroom to hear, 'I just pooped so somebody's going to have to wipe my bum!'"

Rachel's story is a familiar tale of a kid who said too much in a crowded store. She writes, "After two rounds of antibiotics for strep, I got thrush (yeast) in my mouth from being stripped of all the good bacteria. Flash-forward a week later in the grocery store. My seven-year-old son tried to celebrate by saying, 'Yay, your throat is all better but now you have a yeast infection,' quite loudly for all to hear. Of course, I quickly had to clarify, 'Yes, in my throat,' which I'm not sure actually helped my case. I shuffled us out of that aisle and the store pretty quickly after that."

Stacie shares a similar story of public humiliation during a routine run for groceries. She says, "Upon seeing an old priest with an eye patch in the grocery store, my child started pointing and shouting at the top of her lungs, 'Look, Mommy, that guy's a pirate! Mom! A pirate!'"

Road trips with kids are *always* fun. And by *always*, I mean *never*. Anna has quite the reputation at a Taco Bell somewhere in the world. She says, "We were on a road trip and stopped because the two-month-old was hungry. We went into Taco Bell and sat down when the baby was getting really upset. My toddler proceeded to yell, 'Mom, get your boob out!' All the people turned to look at us."

Nicole's story warns that, in the quietness of a library, embarrassing words are really loud. She writes, "After a long day of chasing around after a two-year-old, I groaned a little at my creaky knees as I sat down on a cushion in the library, and my two-year-old said loudly, 'Are you pooing?'" You just never know what their tiny little mouths will spew out next, do you?

Parenting is a tough gig, and it takes time to get the hang of this thing. These next two stories shared by new moms illustrate my point.

Emily and her husband were having a lovely family outing at the park with their new little bundle of joy. Everything was going just peachy until it was time to load the baby up in the car seat. She gives us the warning that they fail to put on strollers: "We had a brand-new baby and went to the park. We drove in the van and brought the stroller. It was time to leave and hubby pushed the stroller over to my side of the van where the baby's car seat was. I was doing something else and hadn't gotten her tiny, sleeping self out of the stroller yet, so when I turned around and saw hubby folding up the stroller and putting it in the van, I assumed he had baby. Nope! He FOLDED OUR BABY UP IN THE STROLLER! We both ran to the back of the van. He grabbed the stroller, unfolded it, and there she was, still peacefully sleeping!"

Then, of course, there's remembering that you have a baby at all! Sheila shares, "In my son's first week of life, I woke up in a panic and yelled, 'Where's the baby?!' My husband woke up, searched the bed, then held up his pillow and declared, 'Here he is!' I looked over to my right in the bassinet and, lo and behold, the baby was safe and sound."

That one cracks me up. Poor dad was so sleepy, he thought the pillow was the baby and *held it up*!

Our tiny humans are so hilarious because they don't mean to be funny most of the time. Jessica shares a story that reminds us all to lock the bathroom door to keep curious children out! She shares, "When my daughter was about two, my husband was getting out of the shower and she happened to walk in. He grabbed his underwear and put them on. A moment later, she says, 'Where did it go?' Husband says, 'Where did what go?' She replies, 'Your tail!' He now showers with the door locked."

When I was a kid, it was always bad news when I got called by my first and middle names at the same time. I wonder if kids who never get in trouble even know their middle names? Karla's kid understands exactly how this works. She says, "My husband and I were talking to our daughter about her first, middle, and last name, Evelyn Florence Thompson. She promptly responded that her name was Evelyn and that she was *only* Evelyn Florence Thompson when she was being bad. She is three."

You know, moms work so hard every day. We just want our kids to eat the meal we prepared without complaining about it. Is that too much to ask? Apparently so. Renée shares, "At the end of a long day, I made a new dinner that my kids were complaining about vociferously. I told them I didn't want to hear any complaining. After a few minutes of silence, my seven-year-old said, 'Mom, this is the yummiest of all your yucky dinners.' I wasn't sure if it was a compliment or not."

Take it as a compliment, Renée. Our kids are pretty good at putting us in our place, lest we get too cocky thinking we are decent cooks or have any talents whatsoever. Hannah writes, "My four-year-old daughter and I were sitting on the couch watching the *Yo Gabba Gabba* "Everybody Has a Talent" episode during quiet time. She stated, 'My talents are riding my bike, swinging, and coloring. Mommy, what's your talent?' 'I'm good at swimming and cooking.' She said, 'And sitting?' Yes, yes. Sitting is a talent of mine."

Do you know what else kids are good at? Calling you out in front of your in-laws. Jamie had an awkward moment at a recent family outing when her son repeated something he'd heard earlier that day. She writes: "At a recent family outing, I was talking to my mother-in-law, my five-year-old sitting next to me. My hubby walked past us following a very excited four-year-old. I commented out loud, 'Look, there goes your dad. Isn't he the best,' which my son piped up with, 'That's not what you said this morning, Mom! You said he was a lazy thing!' Lesson learned. Best whisper when calling hubby names."

Lily's kid is trying to figure out the world. Why do stones appear when you bury someone? He must have pondered it for a while as they were eating. Lily shares, "My four-year-old twins went to Stradbroke Island recently and were eating lunch near the cemetery. Nan was trying to explain that when people die they are sometimes buried. Mr. Four piped up and said oh so seriously, 'Do they then turn into statues?'"

Megan's kid is sharp. And very literal. She says, "My sister took my kids for an afternoon. She was putting on some music in the car and asked my little one, 'What's your favorite jam,' so she could put on something she would like. Kiddo, without missing a beat, yelled 'Strawberry!'" Strawberry is my favorite jam, too, kid! Why would she know that we sometimes call music "jam"? Our language is very confusing for kids.

Sometimes, the sheer randomness of their words makes our tiny humans so hilarious. Elizabeth says, "My seven-year-old daughter got up exceptionally late one day. She popped out of bed and looked at the clock and said, 'Wow! 9:24! New high score!'" I guess life really is like a video game!

Life with kids often leaves us puzzled, but not often does it leave us stuck as a noodle. Leanne shares, "My son was pretending to be Dracula. He grabs his cape with one hand, covers his face—all but his eyes—in the way that Dracula does, and says, 'Look into my eyes' in his best Dracula voice. This is him hypnotizing me. So I pretend to be entranced and then he says, 'You are now a noodle.' And then he walked away." I mean, his job there was done.

Then there are those rare occasions when your kid says something that makes you a little afraid to go to sleep at night. Ashley writes, "My four-year-old daughter found a pretty red leaf on the ground during a walk this afternoon. She said, 'I love red. It's the color of blood. And Target.'"

I wonder if Ashley's kid is friends with Sidney's daughter? Listen to what she said: "When my child was four, she came into the bathroom while I showered, stared at me for a minute, then said, 'Mom, when you die, your necklaces will be in a pool of blood.' Then she walked away." How cryptic and creepy is that?

Strategy: Giggle Often

It's a simple strategy but an important one. Having a sense of humor makes life more fun! It makes your kids want to hang around you more and is great at connecting people. Laughter is contagious, so the more joyful you are, the more joyful your family will be. Laughter triggers the release of endorphins and, for us older adults (ahem), it has been shown to improve short-term memory. So, I'm hoping that by laughing more, I'll remember why I entered a room.

Happiness Habit

Kids say the funniest things! Record the laugh-out-loud stuff your kid says below.

Journal Prompts

1. Who in your circle of family and friends makes you laugh the most? Why?

2. Write about a funny experience you've had.

3. Exercise your brain and your sense of humor. Make up a joke.

4. What's a funny thing that you've seen another kid do out in public?

5. What television show did you find funny as a kid?

Chapter Seventeen

Setting the Tone for a Joyful Home

I have often heard the phrase that moms set the emotional tone of a home. Our own moods are reflected in the moods of our children. In my experience, this is absolutely true. My kids confess that my mood and attitude greatly affect them and that my happiness is extremely important to them. Moms create the atmosphere our children live and grow in. This is both an incredible pressure and a tremendous privilege.

This means it is now imperative for me to be emotionally mature. You would think that, as an adult, this wouldn't be an issue, but have a look around you. Tantrums and throwing "sticks and stones" at one another is not uniquely a child problem. Social media has effectively become a bully's playground for adults, and just look at a Twitter feed, for goodness' sake. We are an emotionally reactive bunch, to say the least, but we moms must rise above reactivity and learn healthy ways to properly manage our emotions. We have to purposefully choose joy and a positive attitude so that our children can grow and thrive in a happy home. This takes work, and yet if I cannot control my emotions at the age of forty, how on earth can I expect my nine-year-old to control his? Tough truths.

If I take care of my emotional state, I can positively impact my children's emotional states, and that is something truly amazing. I can create an environment where my children feel safe, loved, and worthy. I can make my home a place of belonging, and that is some of our most important work, Mamas. This is holy ground. That's the real reason we take our shoes off when we enter, right? If I get the environment—the tone—in my home wrong, the consequences can be catastrophic. My kids could grow up in an unstable, argumentative, toxic home filled with frustrations and boiling points. However, getting it right means everything.

So, Mama, how can you and I grow in emotional maturity? How can we handle this responsibility of setting the tone in our homes with grace and confidence? First, let's look at the differences in emotional maturity and immaturity:

Emotionally mature:

- Self-awareness of moods and their effects

- Ability to self-regulate

- Actions guided by purpose and vision

Emotionally immature:

* Lack of self-awareness

* Behavior driven by emotions

* Actions governed by habit rather than goals

Growing in Emotional Maturity

The first step in managing our emotional reactions is self-awareness, and this is the ability to recognize and understand moods and emotions and how they affect not only our behavior but also the people around us. For me, learning this has been a process. I used to believe my mood was entirely created by the circumstances or environment I was in, but I've since learned (and am still working on applying) the fact that my mood and my emotions are a direct result of my thoughts, and learning to manage my thoughts has been a big challenge of parenting for me. If I went through my day letting everything my kids do "wrong" frustrate me and throw me into a sour mood, I would be giving away so much joy and, honestly, I'd be giving a lot of power to my children. If I allow hateful comments on social media, piles of laundry, or other minor annoyances dictate my mood, I'm setting myself up for an unhappy life. Self-awareness comes through being mindful, keeping a finger on the pulse of my thoughts and feelings, and adjusting as necessary.

Once we become aware of our emotions and how we handle them, the next thing we must do is learn how to regulate those emotions. This means that we are able to control impulses and moods and to think before acting. It doesn't do much good to have self-awareness if we don't have self-regulation, yet self-awareness is obviously a critical element as we cannot control that which we are not aware of. My favorite tip for self-regulation is placing a hand over my heart as I breathe deeply and repeat a mantra such as "we are okay" before I respond when I feel my agitation rising. During particularly stressful days, I frequently remind myself that "this too shall pass" and I make a point to do some type of yoga, Pilates, or stretching exercise. There are plenty of calming techniques we can use once we become aware of our emotions. The trick is to *expand that space between action and reaction* and find what best works for us in that interim.

Finally, this all must be driven by an internal motivation. I must be governed by my vision and purpose. I must possess an inner vision of what is important to me in motherhood and in life and be guided by that vision. Otherwise, I will blow wherever the wind takes me. I am a huge believer in resetting my mind daily to my vision, and I'm always recommitting to finding joy in the chaos of parenthood. To help me with this, I've written down my *mothering blueprint*—a vision for the parent I want to be and the goals I want to achieve. When I make it a habit to read through this daily, I am much better at staying on track.

Strategy: Draft Your Vision

Writing down my vision of motherhood was a very helpful exercise for me. It really helped me to get my goals on paper and to create a working plan for how to achieve my goals. Becoming happy, emotionally mature mothers is an intentional choice that requires us to stay focused and to renew our minds daily because, as we have talked about throughout this entire book, there is much to deter us from that path. To draft your vision, think about the following questions:

1. What do I want my legacy to be?

2. What are my main goals as a mother?

3. When my children tell their children about the days when they were growing up, what do I want their stories to be?

4. List several words to describe the environment you hope to cultivate in your home.

Happiness Habit

Is there room for you to grow in emotional maturity? I would venture to say that nearly all of us have room for growth, and that's okay. We are all works in progress, but we are moving forward, and that's what matters. Today, think of three or four ways you can regulate your emotions and take control of your own behavior when you feel frustration rising. Write them in the spaces below and then, over the next few days, try each one out and come back to record which works best for you.

Journal Prompts

1. Do you believe you set the emotional tone? Do you see your attitudes reflected in your child's?

2. How do you want your child to deal with his or her emotions, and are you modeling the behavior that you hope to see?

3. What is the single biggest purpose that is driving you?

4. What steps can you begin to take today to see your motherhood vision come to fruition?

5. Draft your mothering blueprint. What is your vision? Your values? Your guiding principles? What goals do you have for your family, yourself, and your children, and how can you achieve those goals? Remember to write down small, actionable steps and read your blueprint regularly to keep yourself on track.

Chapter Eighteen

Act 2: When the Littles Are Suddenly Big

I've noticed something weird. When we have little kids, moms talk to each other about how we're *feeling*. We discuss all those swirling emotions of love, awe, joy, exhaustion, and worry. There's a camaraderie among moms of littles.

When we have big kids, particularly middle school kids, moms talk to each other about what we're *doing*. It's "Oh, we are really busy doing this and doing that," and no one says a peep about all the feelings of parenting kids this age. I think it's time we talk about it!

It hurts like hell.

This is the age when the end comes into sight and it can feel absolutely horrifying. This is the age when you're no longer the center of their universe. They start to pull away, and it's like ripping a Band-Aid off that's been glued to you for eleven years. This is the end of act

1, people, and coming to grips with that is a painful process. Or is it just me? Tell me it's not just me!

This has been a time of reckoning for me. When my littles became big, it hit me like an infant car seat to the hip bone that they wouldn't be under my feet forever. During the year my children turned eleven and nine, I literally had weeks of grieving about this fact. For some reason, my baby boy turning nine was a gut punch. I remember sobbing to my husband about how they were growing up so fast and it was completely unfair and frankly quite disobedient of them, as I'd told them many times to stay small! I cried that I'd *never be so loved again* and it was a raw, beating, deep kind of ache. Still, when I think about it, I fold up into a quivering mess. That's what this really boils down to for me—*never being so loved again.* Oh, my heart. I know they love me, don't get me wrong. They still tell me every day, but let's face it, I'll soon be tossed aside like a bologna string when a new girl steals their hearts.

My husband looked me right in the eyes and said, "Yes, your relationships are going to change, but that's natural and how it should be." The nerve! That's not helping! I know it's *natural,* but it still hurts, okay?

I suspect the reason moms of middle schoolers don't talk about this is fear of judgment. We can hardly say anything in regard to motherhood these days without that fear, it seems. I don't want to sound like I'm too clingy. I don't want to be called names related to flying aircrafts. I'm not keen on being perceived as the needy mom who just can't let her precious snowflake grow up. So I don't tell the other moms about my tears and fears. Instead, I just say, "Yep, we have this tonight, that tomorrow, and another thing on Saturday. So busy!" Then I wonder in secret if they even REALIZE THEIR BABIES ARE HALF GROWN!

Sometimes when my kids are gone somewhere, I'll notice how quiet it is and I'll think, *My God, this is what it's going to be like.* It sounds peaceful for a couple of hours, but then I can't stand it anymore. The silence is deafening. When they get home, I'm so happy to hear their loud chatter echo throughout the house again.

From the moment I knew they existed, I have loved these boys every moment and with every breath. They are my world, and for more than a decade, I have been theirs. I've kissed their scrapes and held their hands. I've been the one they run to, lean on, and talk to. I won't always be their number one, and I've been aware of that fact from the day they were placed in my arms. In fact, one of the first things I did after giving birth to my first son was call my mother-in-law to apologize for taking her son away. I realized at the moment when I held my son for the first time what it must have felt like for her to let my husband go. And now my own letting go is getting close enough for me to see it clearly, and wow. This feels harder than those sleep-deprived days of caring for a newborn, and it seems it's not just me after all!

In a study[7] published in *Developmental Psychology*, psychologists Suniya Luthar and Lucia Ciciolla surveyed more than twenty-two hundred mothers with children ranging in age from infant to early adulthood and found that middle school was the most challenging time for mothers. Their data reflected a gradual but consistent increase in maternal distress that peaks when children are in middle school. Luthar said, "Many mothers aren't aware that the big separation from offspring, the one that really hurts, doesn't occur when children leave the nest, but when they psychologically pull away from their mothers. This is a time of psychological metamorphosis for both mother and child."

Psychological metamorphosis! That's exactly what I'm experiencing. There is a silver lining, though. Here's what else the authors of the study had to say. "Regarding the later years of motherhood, our findings support suggestions that the 'empty nest' syndrome is largely a myth. Mothers of adult children reported the least role overload, and on measures of stress, parenting experiences . . . they fared significantly better than mothers of middle-schoolers." However, study or no study, I've decided not to spend these years distressed because I do have a choice. And so do you.

Wisdom is like rain water; both gather in the low places.
—Tibetan saying

I handled this motherhood evolution like any rational, sane mother would. I ugly cried. I told my dog about how much it hurt to let go a little, how I'd give anything to have chubby toddler arms wrapped around my neck again, how I wish I could still pick them up and rock them in my arms. She cocked her little head to the side, long dachshund ears flopping, and almost looked empathetic. I think she gets me. I ugly cried some more. Ice cream came into play. Then I decided that, yes, act 1 is over, but the show must go on! So I dried up my face, moisturized really well (because, aging!), and got ready to step onstage for act 2.

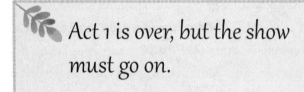

Act 1 is over, but the show must go on.

This transition to life with big kids requires a rearranging of roles and a rediscovering of self. Now I've got to learn when to hold tighter to trust and more loosely to hands. I've got to figure out where I fit in with these small man children. I decided I could forever feel sorry for myself and be sad, thinking my best days were behind me, or I would make more great memories to cherish and enjoy each day with my big kids. My saving realization was that I can choose to be grateful for these years. I can choose to live happy right where I am. I can choose to see through a positive lens. I want to sail through these years with grace, open arms, and an attitude of gratitude because they may not be little anymore, but they're still here with me to love and to enjoy, and that's just what I plan to do. And when the day comes that their bags are packed and they're ready to leave my home, well, I'll just go with them.

Scooch over, darling, and make room for me. You're paying the rent now. Bring me a Diet Coke. Hey, son, I'm hungry. Make me a sandwich?

I kid. Probably.

Living Act 2 with Intention

Generally speaking, there is a three-act structure in playwriting. The first act is the protasis, or exposition, in which the main conflict and characters are revealed. The second act is the epitasis, or complication, in which the plot thickens, peaking at its end. The final act is the catastrophe, or resolution, in which the conflict comes to some kind of conclusion.

In act 1 of motherhood, we meet the characters and spend quite some time getting to know them (and ourselves as moms). During the first decade or so, characters develop and the story unfolds. Act 2 begins, in my mind, when our babies become preteens. This is when the plot thickens, and certainly *complication* feels like a suitable word. It peaks at its end, which is somewhere around high school graduation. The final act, the catastrophe (aptly named), begins when your children become adults. This is the beginning of the conclusion (and pretty much lasts the rest of your life). Yes, I made all of this up in my head, but stick with me, Mamas. If you're not already in act 2, it's coming! This will help you prepare.

It would be easy to sail through this season on autopilot, wouldn't it? Life with big kids involves a lot of running around and getting things done. The family dynamic is different, too. We used to watch a lot of shows and movies together, play board games, and just generally hang out together. We still do a fair amount of those things, but more and more, they are into their own hobbies and following their own interests. Our once slow and easy weekends are filled with our kids' friends, ball games, and school projects that never seem to end. The point is, it's not as easy to spend quality time together as it was when they were little, and if I want positive relationships with my preteens and teens, if I want to seek out joy in act 2, I have to be intentional about it.

Strategy: Step Onstage

I admit, occasionally there is a part of me that wants to slink back in the curtains and wish for days gone by, but here we are. There is no going back, so I've decided to step onstage and give it my very best shot. This is my five-habit plan for cultivating happiness in this stage of motherhood.

Speak Life

More than ever, my children need me to speak life-giving, affirming words to them. They need my unwavering belief in their goodness and capabilities. Adolescence is a time of uncertainty, of figuring out where you fit. I need my boys to know they'll always fit perfectly at home. I need them to feel certain of my love when they feel certain of little else.

I feel that this is an important time to speak *into who my kids are becoming*. Even as big kids, their brains still have a lot of developing to do. There is still much growth to occur, and my job isn't finished yet. I can affirm their strengths even when I see their weaknesses. I can affirm their courage even when I see their fear. I can affirm their wisdom even when I see a poor decision.

As moms, our words have so much power. If you still have your mother's voice in your head, you know this to be true. Whether your own mother was an encouragement or a discouragement to you, it's likely that you still feel the effects years later. My children will always hear my voice to some extent, and I want to make sure the voice they hear serves them well.

Send Them Off and Greet Them with Love

If my kids and I part on unhappy terms in the morning, I feel like a cloud hangs over my day. I wonder if they feel that way, too. When mornings are rushed and it takes a lucky streak of green traffic lights to make it to school before the bell, a less mindful me will send them off with "Hurry up! Go!" That's not a great way to start the school day. Spending five more seconds isn't going to make a significant difference in getting to class on time, but it means I can connect with my child and send him off to his day on a positive note. I can do this by taking the extra time to say, "I hope you have a great day and I can't wait to see you this afternoon! I love you!" The last words our loved ones say to us often linger, so try to make them happy words!

A kind and loving greeting after a period of separation is another mindfulness habit that has a positive effect on the relationship. When my kids rejoin me after a night of sleep, a day of school, or even a short separation, I want to greet them with warmth and enthusiasm because it conveys two strong messages. The first is that you are important enough for me to look up from my phone or my work or give you focused attention and the second is that I genuinely like seeing you and being around you.

These two small practices, sending off with love and greeting with love, can be done all throughout the day and serve as little connection points. Even if my kid has just been in his room watching TV for a while and comes into the room where I am, I try to make a point to look up and acknowledge him with a smile. It's a small way that I can make my children feel loved and significant, and that makes us all feel happier.

My 3-1-1 Rule

As I've said, life with big kids is hectic. Some days, it feels like everyone is going in different directions. It's important to me that I stay connected to my kids, and that we spend quality time as a family. To ensure this happens, I've made a 3-1-1 rule. We eat together in our dining room at least three days a week, we go out for dinner together once a week (the kids pick the restaurant), and we set aside at least one night a week for a family activity.

Our dinner conversations allow us to hear what's going on in their worlds. It provides opportunities for us to tell our kids stories of our childhood experiences so that they relate to us. Family activities give us a chance to play together, to laugh, and to bond. Moms, we have to be purposeful about keeping our kids emotionally close. That's the only way we will maintain any influence now that we are competition with so many other influences in our big kids' lives. When I put quality time on our calendar, we honor it just as we would any other appointment.

Delight in Who They Are Today

As Stacia Tauscher said, "We worry what a child will become to-morrow, yet we forget that he is someone today." Those are wise words, indeed. I have these words pinned to my board in my bedroom to remind me that *who my child is today needs to be celebrated*. I want my kids to know that I delight in who they are right now, and I ask you, is there a better gift than to feel like you're good as is? Another favorite quote of mine comes from Glennon Doyle. She says, "Don't let yourself become so concerned with raising a good kid that you forget you already have one."

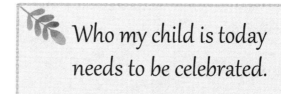

Who my child is today
needs to be celebrated.

I can show my kids that I delight in them by speaking affirming words, being present and engaged when I'm spending time with them, and also apparently by watching "try not to laugh" videos on YouTube. It's the simple things, really, that mean so much to kids. When I delight in who they are right now, I'm experiencing just that—*delight*!

Make Big Memories

When it dawned on me that I only had a few more summers with my firstborn before he potentially heads to college or the workforce, I freaked out just a little bit. I upped my game on family vacations, weekend getaways, and special outings. We do more double features at the movies with giant bags of popcorn, and we frequent the trampoline park and the skating rink. Why? Frankly, I'm trying to cram in tons of big, wonderful memories.

When I look back on my childhood, I don't remember a thing about being three. I have no idea what we did together when I was seven. The memories that stand out in my mind all happened when I was in the preteen/teen years. Those memories are what I gauge my childhood by. So even though all of the years leading up to this point were so important in shaping who my children are and will become, I also realize that these are the days that will define *childhood* in their minds. The memories we make over the next few years are the ones that will be at the forefront of their minds when they think of *home* and *family*. I intend on giving them lots of joyful memories to choose from.

Happiness Habit

How can you step onstage right now? I just listed five happiness habits that will help me live and love my best during act 2. You can borrow one of these or come up with your own, but think of one way you can squeeze a bit of joy out of the season you are in and commit to your new happy habit. Write it here.

_____

_____

_____

Journal Prompts

1. What has been the most surprising part of motherhood so far?

2. Which season do you miss the most?

3. What's great about your child right now?

4. Name one place you hope to visit with your kids before they are grown.

5. What is one thing you're going to miss about this stage you are in?

On Turning Forty

It just so happens that, at the same time my littles are becoming big, I'm turning the big 4-0. Age is a funny thing. I remember my parents turning forty and thinking they were *ancient*. There were "over the hill" balloons and all that. I couldn't imagine being so old, but suddenly here I am, and I don't *feel old*. Well, not mentally anyway. My back aches a lot and I creak when I stand up. My hormones are out of whack and I have lines in my forehead that make me look permanently surprised, which probably comes from raising my eyebrows a bajillion times at my kids.

The days of my youth have gone by. In my twenties, my eyes were brighter and I didn't sprout gray hairs, but I'm ragged and worn a bit now. I've been loved *real good*. Like the Velveteen Rabbit or a child's favorite lovey, my body shows definite signs of wear, but I can look in the mirror and smile because I know I've meant the world to two little boys. Growing older is really a beautiful thing, but of course, it all depends on your mind-set.

There is this mental shift that I'm experiencing that is really difficult to put into words. I don't feel *older*. I feel *freer*. I've always had an old soul, and I suppose now it finally feels at home in my "old" body. I feel *settled in*. Just as I spoke about a psychological metamorphosis in motherhood when little children become big, it seems to me there is also a kind of personal metamorphosis that happens around forty, except I have emerged from my cocoon with batwings rather than butterfly wings. Not cute, furry bats, mind you. Arm jiggle. There's sort of a comfort in my (more dimpled and wrinkled) skin, though, that I didn't feel in my twenties or thirties.

This midlife thing is actually pretty cool, in many ways. I can go to bed early now without an excuse. There are no party invitations to have to decline. While it's true that hairs are sprouting in odd places, I can't really see them without glasses, so it doesn't matter anyway. Losing weight is harder but I care less. I figure my time to enter modeling is long past anyway, so I eat the cupcake and life is good. I know who my real friends are, and while I don't have as many as I used to,

I know these girls are the real deal. When you're forty, you don't have time for fake friends.

You realize at forty that you don't have forever. You're not invincible. Time is borrowed and it's always running out. There is no more time for wasted dreams, keeping quiet, toxic people, drama, lettuce diets, people pleasing, or settling for less than you deserve. So you sit down and start writing that book you always wanted to write. You speak your mind because you no longer care what everyone's opinion of you is. You know your voice is just as important as everyone else's. You let the people go who drain your energy because there's only a small reserve of it as it is. You rise above the petty, immature stuff of your youth and it feels good to be on the open high road. You make more time for the things you enjoy and the people you love because it's all a little more precious now somehow. You're forty, and life just got real. You ain't playing no more.

Age is a gift. Turning forty is a gift. I intend to live act 2 and, after that, my final act, with purpose, enthusiasm, and with joy. I do not choose to sit here and wait to die. I choose to keep on dreaming, to keep on growing, and to keep on living my life to the fullest. Maya Angelou's words are an inspiration to me in this stage of my life. "My mission in life is not merely to survive, but to thrive; and to do so with some passion, some compassion, some humor, and some style."

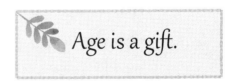

Age is a gift.

Allow me to share some of my favorite quotes on turning forty. They make me smile. They make me laugh. They make me feel grateful. To my midlife mamas, here's to you.

Life begins at forty—but so do fallen arches, rheumatism,
faulty eyesight, and the tendency to tell a story to
the same person three or four times.
—Helen Rowland

I'd rather be forty than pregnant.
—Karen Kavet

You know you're turning forty when the light from your
birthday cake candles significantly contribute to global warming.
—Linda Klemanski

We don't understand life any better at forty than at twenty,
but we know it and admit it.
—Jules Renard

Forty years old—the halfway point between
diapers and Depends.
—Unknown

The best part of being forty is that we did most
of our stupid stuff before the Internet.
—Unknown

Strategy: Radical Gratitude

We have all heard how important gratitude is, and we know that being thankful for the good things in our lives is good for our mental health and happiness. It's not hard to be happy for the good things, though. It may take presence and focus to notice them, but once we do, it's definitely not hard to appreciate goodness. What is more difficult is appreciating challenges, setbacks, or things we may not necessarily deem "good." Yet, isn't there purpose in those as well?

I've written in plenty of gratitude journals, and up until now, they've always been the same. I'm grateful for my kids. I'm grateful for my husband. I'm grateful for our health. I'm grateful for the beautiful sunset. I'm grateful for the nice weather. I always express gratitude for my blessings, and that's a wonderful thing, but I want to grow in this idea of radical gratitude. I want to see the benefit in the struggle. I want to open my eyes and my heart to the hidden goodness that may come cloaked in hardship or even pain.

This doesn't mean that I'm thankful *for* bad circumstances. It means that I'm thankful *in* them. It means that I choose to look for the silver lining, and if I can find none there, then I will choose to still be grateful. Radical gratitude is having appreciation for life even when life isn't going my way. I figure if I can master that, then I will truly be the master of my own happiness.

Happiness Habit

Practice radical gratitude with me. Name three difficult, unpleasant, painful, or challenging things that have happened (or are happening) in your life that you are grateful for.

1.

_____

_____

_____

2.

_____

_____

_____

3.

_____

_____

_____

Journal Prompts

1. What would you do if you only had one month left to live?

2. How have you grown because of a certain hardship in your life?

3. Have you lost someone dear to you? If you could speak to that person one more time, what would you say?

4. What is the best thing about growing older?

5. Name an older person you admire.

Chapter Nineteen

The Quilt of Life

The rain poured down in sheets from the dark gray clouds just as it had done for the past three days. The sky was purging itself of all its heaviness. Of all the storms she'd seen over her many decades, this one, she thought, was one of the most beautiful. The silver spikes drove straight into the pavement and splashed back up in cheerful bursts. She watched the drops shimmy and race down the window, and she smiled. It seemed the rain had come to play. The deluge hammered against the metal roof, sounding like a thousand footsteps marching to the beat, and the sound made her sleepy. She thought to herself that it would be very nice to take a nap once her work was finished.

She adjusted her glasses and went back to work, carefully hand-stitching a quite beautiful square of fabric, an Ohio Star pattern in vibrant blues and greens. The colors reminded her of hiking in the mountains in her youth with the clear blue sky ahead and the thick, luscious forest of trees all around. She was putting the final stitches in on a project that had taken her so much time to create, and finally it was nearly done. She could see the beauty she had created, and her heart was glad at the sight of it.

She slowly stood and shuffled to the kitchen for a refill of tea. The filled teapot sat on the burner already, so she turned on the heat and went for her tea bag. The cupboard door sighed with a quiet squeak as she closed it. Taking a knife from the block and slicing off a corner brownie, she chided herself about the sugar but was unable to convince herself of putting the brownie back in the pan. She deserved a little treat, after all. She had been working hard all morning to get it ready. The shrill whistling from the teapot startled her. It always did, even after six decades of making tea. She laughed at her skittishness and caught a shadow passing by the window as she turned to take the pot off the stove. Seconds later, the doorbell rang.

"Hello, love! Hello!" She swung the door open wide and embraced him. Another car door shut and the sound of little feet splashing through the puddles was such a delight that her smile broadened even more. "Hurry in out of the rain," she said, and the little girl ran up to her and threw her arms around her neck as she bent down to greet her. "Grandma!" she said excitedly. "We saw ducks on the way here!" Her big brown eyes were wide with excitement. *Those eyes,* she thought to herself. Those big chocolate brown eyes had been inherited from her father, and his father before him, and they were magnificent. "You did? Wonderful! Please come in, dear. I have brownies!"

The two came inside and placed the dripping wet umbrella in the corner. She welcomed a little mess. "Where's Dad?" the man asked. Brown Eyes and his brother came by regularly, each visit filling the old mama's heart a little more. "At the garage," she said with her head tilted to glance above her glasses. They gave each other a knowing chortle. Grandpa loved tinkering over there, always keeping busy. The little girl took notice of the heap beside the rocking chair and said, "Oh, that's pretty! When did you get it?" With hands tired from hours of stitching, she took the quilt into her lap and smoothed out the crinkles. "Do you like it? I made this for you." She pushed herself up from the chair and let the quilt fully open, cascading down to the floor in vivid colors and spirited patterns. "For me?" Little Brown Eyes asked in wonderment, and she clapped her hands in happiness. "Yes," Grandma said, "for you." The little girl took the quilt in her hands and studied it, square by square, her eyes dancing over the designs. "Wow! It's so beautiful, Grandma. How did you make it?" Her eyes glistened as tears of joy sprang up at her granddaughter's joy. "Why, one square at a time, of course."

A happy life is made of a million little happy moments all stitched together with great purpose. Like the quilt that takes so many hours of choosing fabrics, deliberate sewing, and careful binding to make splendid, so does your quilt of life—the moments, days, and seasons of your years patched together to reveal the beauty of all you have done. Each time you choose joy over fear, guilt, anger, comparison, judgment, or any of the happiness stealers, you are adding beauty to your quilt.

In the opening of this book, I told you about my son and how his biggest wish is that his mother is happy. I didn't understand what my own joy meant to my children, though I should have realized the importance of it just by looking back on my own childhood. Our parents' happiness or unhappiness seeps into the corners of our own hearts. We were undeniably affected by their joys and sorrows, and now our joys and sorrows undeniably affect our own kids. When I choose happiness, I am giving my child the gift of a happy mother. There is nothing that money can buy that will be so important or so impactful.

I am not a finished product. I have much more growing and learning to do, even at my advanced maternal age. Hopefully, I still have a lot of squares to make, but I'm happy with how this one is turning out. I have made progress throughout these many months on my happiness journey, and I pray that you're seeing some progress, too. When I look at Brown Eyes now, I like the reflection I see now better than before. That's something.

I hope that, as you have turned these pages, you've found a way to love yourself better. I hope you've found the path to self-acceptance and the courage to release your guilt. I hope you triumph over fear and darkness and that you see a reflection of joy when you look in the eyes of your precious one. I hope the square you're stitching today is one you'll remember as significant and exquisite when you one day look over your quilt of life.

Sisters, I want you to remember this: Every season is significant, every day adds beauty, and every moment is another stitch placed, but not all the stitches have to be perfect and not all squares have to be glorious for the quilt to end up amazing. Certainly there is room for a few mistakes in the making of it and it can still keep you warm at

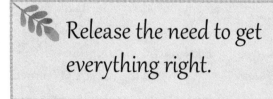

Release the need to get everything right.

night. Let go of the pressure to be perfect. Release the need to get everything right. Give yourself permission to be human, and embrace your flawed, wonderful self. I know you want your kids to do the same. Things don't have to be perfect to be really, really good.

Strategy: Focus on the Square You're Stitching

We moms have the tendency to focus our eyes on the future, anticipating what may come and trying to plan for it. Some of us tend to focus our eyes on the past, regretting and wishing we could change it somehow. It does us no good to focus on tomorrow's square or yesterday's square. Who knows what will happen tomorrow? We might decide on completely new fabric then. Who can change what happened yesterday? Those ugly squares will remind us of how much we've overcome. It's really best just to focus on the square we're on today. It's too important to take our eyes off of. Tomorrow will take care of itself if we just stay focused on doing our best today at loving well and collecting joy.

My aging fingers ache, so I'm going to close out this book with one final word. Well, one final paragraph. As I sit here in this wonderful, awkward crossroad of midlife, forty and fabulous, I have two last pieces of advice. One: Go ahead and invest in a good facial hair remover. Two: Heed the words of Mother Teresa: "Yesterday is gone. Tomorrow has not yet come. We have only today. Let us begin."

Happiness Habit

Time teaches us many lessons. One valuable lesson I've learned during my time as a mother is not to sweat the small things. Children develop in their own time. One of the reasons I was often looking to the next stage was because I was anxious that my child was "behind" and I would get my stomach in knots worrying if he'd catch up. We worry too much about reading levels, potty training, and messy rooms and perhaps too little about living a happy life with our loved ones in the short time we are given with them.

What is one small thing that you need to stop sweating over?

_____

_____

_____

Journal Prompts

1. What do you want the future elderly you to know about who you are today?

2. What is the next "big thing" you want to do in your life?

3. This square that you're on now, how is it looking? How can you improve it?

4. Write about something you did really well this week and something you could have done better.

5. What is the one thing that struck you the most as you read this book? Make a note of it.

Notes

1   Nancy Shute, "To Succeed at Breast-Feeding, Most New Moms Could Use Help," NPR, September 23, 2013, www.npr.org/sections/health-shots/2013/09/23/225349120/to-succeed-at-breast-feeding-most-new-moms-could-use-help.

2   Keith Wagstaff, "Happiness Equation Solved: Lower Your Expectations," TODAY.com, August 4, 2014, www.today.com/health/happiness-equation-solved-lower-your-expectations-1D80018852.

3   Kelly Turner, "The Science Behind Intuition," *Psychology Today, Radical Remission* (blog), May 20, 2014, https://www.psychologytoday.com/blog/radical-remission/201405/the-science-behind-intuition (accessed January 31, 2018).

4   DeCesare, Melissa. "Moms and Media 2017: the Highlights." *Edison Research*, Edison Research. February 12, 2018, www.edisonresearch.com/moms-media-2017-highlights/.

5   Darcia Narvaez, "Happiness and Growth Through Play," *Psychology Today, Moral Landscapes* (blog), March 29, 2014, www

.psychologytoday.com/blog/moral-landscapes/201403/hap
piness-and-growth-through-play.

6   Noam Shpancer, "How to Stop Worrying and Get On with Your
     Life," *Psychology Today*, *Insight Therapy* (blog), January 2, 2015,
     www.psychologytoday.com/blog/insight-therapy/201501/how
     -stop-worrying-and-get-your-life.

7   Suniya S. Luthar and Lucia Ciciolla, "What It Feels Like to Be
     a Mother: Variations by Children's Developmental Stages,"
     Developmental Psychology 52, no. 1 (January 2016): 143–54,
     www.ncbi.nlm.nih.gov/pmc/articles/PMC4695277/.

Acknowledgments

We know that it takes a village to raise a child, and likewise it takes a village to create a book. I want to acknowledge my village with a heartfelt thank-you. I have been incredibly fortunate to find a community of writers, authors, coaches, and therapists who have supported and inspired me since I was a fledgling blogger. There are too many to list, but for each of you in my various online groups who have collaborated and shared and encouraged, thank you so much.

To my dear friends, Bridgett Miller and Lelia Schott, you have no idea how much you mean to me. Thank you for your love and support.

To my agent, Sandra Bishop, and my team at TarcherPerigee—Marian Lizzi, Roshe Anderson, Dani Harris, and others working behind the scenes—I am forever grateful for your wisdom, guidance, and vision. Thank you for sending my voice out into the world.

To the members of my Facebook community and readers around the world, thank you for allowing me into your lives, for reading my words and listening to my voice. Thank you for giving me the platform to spread my messages of unfailing love, kindness to all, and joy in our ordinary days. I hope I've made at least a small positive difference in your life. Your encouragement and support mean so much to me.

To Roma, Walter, Trudy, Trent, Stephanie, Jamie, and Amanda, I'm so grateful God made me a part of this family. Thank you for loving me like a daughter and a sister. I love you all.

To my parents, many thanks for all you have done for me.

To my husband, you have been a constant source of strength and encouragement, and I am forever grateful to share life with you. Thank you for believing in all of my wild dreams. I love you so much.

To Gavin, you are a tremendous gift to me. Your light has touched so many people, and I'm blessed to be your mom. Thank you for showing me the way toward greater compassion and gentleness. The world is lucky to have you, and it was an honor for me to bring you to it. I love you to the moon.

To Aiden, life wouldn't be the same without your vibrant energy and laughter. You've brought so much joy into my life. I'm so lucky to be your mom! Thank you for giving me the gift of happiness and un-conditional love. My soul needed you. I love you more than cake.

About the Author

Rebecca Eanes is the founder of positive-parents.org and creator of the Facebook community Positive Parenting with Rebecca Eanes. She is the author of *The Newbie's Guide to Positive Parenting, Positive Parenting: An Essential Guide*, and *The Positive Parenting Workbook*, and coauthor of *Positive Parenting in Action*. She is a parenting editor at *Motherly* and contributing editor to *Creative Child* magazine and *Baby Maternity Magazine*. She is a certified Parent Coach from the Jai Institute of Parenting.

Rebecca has been writing for six years, in the middle of motherhood and mayhem, to speak to hearts around the globe with encouragement and inspiration. Often taking to her laptop in the wee hours while her children slumbered, sleep deprivation has been no obstacle for sharing her passions with the world. She does, however, plan to take a two-year nap when her last child leaves her nest.

She is married to her high school sweetheart and is nestled against the beautiful Appalachian Mountains with her two sons, two comical pooches, and a growing number of stray cats.

You are invited to join her tribe on Facebook at Positive Parenting with Rebecca Eanes, online at positive-parents.org and rebeccaeanes.com, and subscribe to her newsletter to receive exclusive video content, freebies, and more.

ALSO BY REBECCA EANES

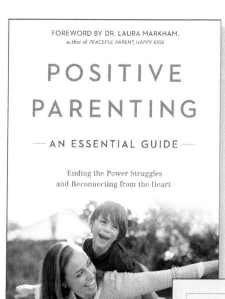

FOREWORD BY DR. LAURA MARKHAM,
author of *PEACEFUL PARENT, HAPPY KIDS*

POSITIVE
PARENTING

— AN ESSENTIAL GUIDE —

Ending the Power Struggles
and Reconnecting from the Heart

REBECCA EANES, Creator of Positive-

THE
POSITIVE
PARENTING
WORKBOOK

An Interactive Guide for
Strengthening Emotional Connection

Rebecca Eanes
Author of *POSITIVE PARENTING* and creator of Positive-Parents.org